Philosophy for Young Children

With this book, any teacher can start teaching philosophy to children today!

Co-written by a professor of philosophy and a practising primary school teacher, *Philosophy for Young Children* is a concise, practical guide for teachers. It contains detailed session plans for 36 philosophical enquiries – enough for a year's work – that have all been successfully tried, tested and enjoyed with young children from the age of three upwards.

The enquiries explore a range of stimulating philosophical questions about fairness, the environment, friendship, inclusion, sharing, right and wrong, manners, beauty, pictures, the emotions, dreaming and reality. All the stories, drawings and photographs that you will need to carry out the enquiries are provided and can be used with your children directly from the book.

Each step-by-step enquiry includes:

- the philosophical topic and the aim of the enquiry
- the stimuli you will need
- questions to ask the children
- possible answers to help move the discussion forward
- ideas to help you summarise and extend the enquiry.

If you are an early years or primary school teacher, this complete resource will enable you to introduce philosophy to your children quickly and with confidence.

Berys Gaut is Professor of Philosophy at the University of St Andrews, UK.

Morag Gaut is a teacher at Anstruther Primary School, Fife, UK.

Philosophy for Young Children

A Practical Guide

Berys Gaut and Morag Gaut

Illustrations by Suzanne Crawford

Routledge
Taylor & Francis Group

LONDON AND NEW YORK

First published 2012
by Routledge
2 Park Square, Milton Park, Abingdon, Oxon OX14 4RN

Simultaneously published in the USA and Canada
by Routledge
711 Third Avenue, New York, NY 10017

Routledge is an imprint of the Taylor & Francis Group, an informa business

British Library Cataloguing in Publication Data
A catalogue record for this book is available from the British Library

Library of Congress Cataloging in Publication Data

Gaut, Berys Nigel.

Philosophy for young children : a practical guide / Berys Gaut and
Morag Gaut.

     p. cm.

    1. Children and philosophy. 2. Philosophy–Study and teaching
(Primary) I. Gaut, Morag. II. Title.

    B105.C45G38 2012

    372.8–dc22   2011006137

ISBN: 978-0-415-61973-8 (hbk)
ISBN: 978-0-415-61974-5 (pbk)
ISBN: 978-0-203-81842-8 (ebk)

Typeset in Bembo
by HWA Text and Data Management, London
Printed and bound by CPI Group (UK) Ltd, Croydon, CR0 4YY

Contents

Introduction

This book is a practical guide to teaching philosophy to young children, from the age of three upwards. It provides not only detailed enquiry plans but also stories and pictures to use in the enquiries. All the enquiries have been used in the classroom, and they are co-written by a practising primary school teacher and a professional philosopher, so they are both practical and philosophically sound. There are 36 enquiries, enough to cover a school year if you use one a week, though we have also used them successfully at less frequent intervals. In this Introduction we'll explain the benefits of philosophy, what philosophy is, and how to use the enquiries that comprise the rest of the book.

Any teacher can teach philosophy

Do not worry if you do not have a philosophy background, this is not necessary to teach philosophy to young children. Teaching philosophy to children of this age involves providing them with the opportunity to engage in philosophical discussion, with you, as the facilitator, keeping the discussion focused. The enquiry plans show you how to lead the discussion. Each plan gives the philosophical aim of the enquiry, provides a stimulus (a story, pictures or an activity), several questions, possible answers and a summary to help you bring out the philosophical issues. So if you follow the enquiry plan you can be confident that you are teaching philosophy. After you have gained in experience, you will be ready to devise your own enquiries along similar lines. For instance, you could keep the questions the same, but change the stories or remove the props, which you may wish to do for enquiries with children in the upper primary school – the questions, answers and reasons work just as well for them. Ideas for an alternative version have been added at the end of some enquiries as examples of how to do this. For instance, we wrote a story about a twins' birthday party, as a variation of The Teddy Bears' Picnic (Chapter 1) and kept the same questions and summary.

Philosophy and the curriculum

Philosophy can include all areas of the curriculum. Using the enquiries in this book will cover many literacy aspects of the curriculum, teach thinking skills and foster independent learning. The enquiries include areas of the curriculum about citizenship, such as fairness (Chapter 1) and the environment (Chapter 2). They also cover emotional (Chapter 6), social (Chapter 3), and personal and moral (Chapter 4) development; the expressive arts (Chapter 5); and even science (A Stick in the Water in Chapter 7). Several enquiries ask the children to vote and then to analyse how they voted, so the children also use information gathering and mathematical skills.

The benefits of philosophy

There are numerous benefits to children from engaging in philosophy and you will begin to see some of them quite rapidly.

During a philosophy enquiry the children can operate at their own level and through discussion develop their ability to think and reason with others. This helps to build the children's self esteem and confidence, as they can all achieve a feeling of success.

The children will also become more active and independent learners. Although you present them with the stimulus and the question, they can take the discussion in a direction which interests them, using their own experience and knowledge to discuss the question.

By doing philosophy children develop many skills. These include:

- critical reasoning skills: giving reasons, assessing objections and counterexamples, finding principles and making distinctions;
- creative thinking skills: coming up with their own ideas and developing them through discussion;
- concentration skills: increasing the length of time that a child can concentrate;
- listening skills: listening carefully and not interrupting when others are speaking;
- communication skills: being able to put their thoughts into words and convey them clearly to others;
- social skills: taking turns and being respectful and tolerant of the ideas of others.

Philosophical questions

Philosophy has two aspects: a set of questions that comprise philosophical topics and a method for answering these questions.

Philosophical questions are fundamental ones, such as how we ought to live, what is right and wrong, how we know whether things really exist, and so on. These kinds of questions have no settled answers, unlike scientific questions and many questions that arise in ordinary life. Different branches of philosophy ask different kinds of questions. For instance:

- political philosophy includes questions about how to distribute things fairly: for instance, whether things should be distributed equally or according to need;
- environmental philosophy includes questions about how we ought to treat the environment: for instance, about the extent to which we ought to build on green land;
- social philosophy includes questions about communities and friendship: for instance, about when we should cooperate with others and the characteristics of a good friend;
- ethics includes questions about virtues and vices, and what is morally right and wrong: for instance, about what kindness is and whether lying is always wrong;
- aesthetics includes questions about beauty and art: for instance, what makes something beautiful, and the differences between photographs and drawings;
- philosophy of mind includes questions about persons and mental states: for instance, what makes someone a person and the nature of the emotions;

- epistemology includes questions about knowledge: for instance, how we know that we are not dreaming;
- metaphysics includes questions about what is real and about when things remain the same: for instance, whether numbers are real and whether something can remain the same even when all of its parts are replaced.

If you look at the table of contents, you will find chapters on all of these areas of philosophy.

Philosophy and reasons

The second aspect of philosophy is a method for answering these kinds of questions. This aspect comprises critical reasoning. Philosophy looks for reasons in support of answers: merely asserting something is not enough. We are familiar in ordinary life with giving reasons, especially when we agree or disagree with others. If you say something, you might support it with an example; and if you disagree with what someone has said, you might give a counterexample, that is, an example that contradicts what the other person has said. Counterexamples are one kind of objection that can be raised to someone's claims: for instance, you might also give an argument for why you disagree and offer arguments in support of your own position. You could also try to find a principle, which is a general kind of reason, to support what you say. And then someone might offer a counterexample to your principle, and you will have to consider whether to abandon your principle, and so change your mind, or you might instead argue that the counterexample is not a good one. Or you might argue that the other person has confused two cases, so a distinction needs to be made between them. Philosophy uses the same sorts of reasoning as we employ in ordinary life but tries to be very careful, clear and systematic in the way it gives reasons and formulates its claims. Young children, even as young as three, can learn to reason in surprisingly sophisticated ways, and you will find many examples of giving reasons in this book, which will help to improve their ability to think independently.

Philosophy and non-philosophy

It is easy to confuse non-philosophical questions and methods with philosophical ones. If you ask the children, 'How would you like to divide the cake?', this is not a philosophical question, since it merely asks them what they would like to do and it doesn't ask them for any reasons. But if you ask them, 'How would it be fair to divide the cake?' and then ask them to give reasons, this is a philosophical question and method. They are now talking about fairness (a topic in political philosophy) and have to give reasons (philosophical method).

Philosophy addresses some fundamental questions and it does so by reasoning about them. Though the philosophy in the enquiries in this book is of course adapted to the abilities of young children, it is genuine philosophy. Teaching it encourages children to think for themselves about questions that they will find very interesting and quite natural to ask, and they will sometimes come up with new and surprising views.

The range of the enquiries

The enquiries are suitable for a range of ages and abilities. They range from reasonably straightforward enquiries which look at topics in ethics, e.g., Pancake the Greedy Rabbit (Chapter 4) to more challenging ones, e.g., Theseus's Ship (Chapter 8), which discusses when things are the same. The enquiries can be used in any order. The children's progress in philosophy will come from them thinking about the questions and so deepening their understanding of the philosophical issues raised, and by developing their critical abilities, rather than by proceeding through the topics in a set order. You may find that some of the youngest children have difficulty with some of the counterexamples and objections, and with some enquiries, e.g., Dreaming of School (Chapter 7) and Theseus's Ship. This does not mean that you should not use them with the younger children, and we have – you may be very pleasantly surprised with their responses.

Several enquiries raise issues that are interconnected. For instance, Teddy's Friends, and William and Arthur (both Chapter 3) are about different aspects of friendship; and Charlotte the Lazy Caterpillar (Chapter 4) refuses to help, as do Gavin's friends in Gavin Builds a Sandpit (Chapter 1). The children will sometimes spot these interconnections and you should encourage them to do so.

Two of the enquiries raise questions that you may feel uncomfortable discussing with some children. School Rules (Chapter 1) asks the children to consider whether they should always obey a school rule and Kirsty (Chapter 4) asks whether we should always tell the truth. These are examples of how philosophy encourages people to question their assumptions. If you feel uncomfortable using them, you do not need to do so. Likewise, if you have doubts about using any of the objections or counterexamples in the enquiries, there is no need to use them. There are plenty of other enquiries, objections and counterexamples to use!

Introducing philosophy to children

When introducing philosophy to your children for the first time you will need to take some time to explain to them what they will be doing during a philosophy enquiry. Even saying and remembering the word 'philosophy' is hard to begin with for some children so you will need to discuss the word itself first. You can then tell them, for example: 'During philosophy we are going to be thinking and talking about lots of different things. We are going to listen to a story and then I will ask you a question which we will talk about. It is very important that you think hard, listen to the others in the group and that only one person speaks at a time.'

You should then explain to the children the rules of a philosophy enquiry. The important ones are:

- Think before you speak.
- Listen to the other children.
- Only one person is to talk at a time.
- Respect other children's opinions.
- Decide whether you agree or disagree with what has been said.
- Give reasons for your answers.

Examples of Philosophy Helpers

To make this fun for the children and to quickly recap at the beginning of an enquiry we have devised Philosophy Helpers. There is a Helper for each rule. They can be shown at the beginning of an enquiry and then put on the floor in the middle of the circle to remind the children of the rules. The children will soon learn to pick up one of the Helpers to show to another child who is not following the rules. You can easily make your own Helpers on a computer or by drawing them yourself.

You should also encourage the children to use the language of a philosophical enquiry. All children should be introduced to the following phrases:

- 'I agree with (child's name) because …'
- 'I disagree with (child's name) because …'
- 'I think … because …'
- 'Why do you think …?'
- 'Can you give a reason?'

You may also wish to introduce, particularly to the older children, some of the other vocabulary that we discussed in the section about philosophy and reasons:

- 'Can you give an example?'
- 'A counterexample to that is …'
- 'I have an objection to …'
- 'Can you state a principle for this?'
- 'Can you generalise that?'
- 'Can you make a distinction here?'

Layout of the enquiry plans

The enquiry plans follow a standard format, with some variations, so you can quickly begin to do philosophy and explore different answers to the philosophical questions raised.

The first heading in the plan is the philosophical topic, which states the branch of philosophy and the particular area within it that the enquiry is about. The aim of the enquiry is given next. The statements of the topic and the aim are for your use and do not need to be read to the children. Next comes the list of props, if any; and then, if there is a story, the story heading. The stories, photographs and drawings you will need are all provided in the enquiry plan. Some stories are given in sections in the main body of the enquiry, and a question is asked after each part of the story. Other stories are placed at the end of the enquiry, and in these cases the questions are asked after you have read the complete story to the children.

The first question is listed next. We provide possible answers to the great majority of the questions. Often we provide a choice between 'if the children answer yes' and 'if the children answer no', so that you can explore both options. The next question usually asks why the children have answered as they did, and we list possible reasons (a reason is an answer to a why question). The reasons and answers are possible ones, in the sense that they are ones that the children may give, but there are many other ways in which the children may respond! In a few cases we talk of answers, rather than possible answers, since these are answers to straightforward questions about what happened in the story.

In response to many reasons and answers we give objections and counterexamples. A counterexample is a type of example, whereas an objection is more general. The counterexamples are often put by asking questions to which the children are likely to answer in a way that creates the counterexample; e.g., in Sam's Kind Day (Chapter 4) most children will say that we should always be kind to others, and the counterexample is to ask them whether they should be kind to someone who is being nasty to them. Some counterexamples and objections are to a particular reason, in which case they are placed after that reason; others are to how the children have responded to the question, in which case they are at the end of the list of reasons (see Sam's Kind Day). In some cases we provide follow up questions: if they are a follow up to a particular reason they are placed after the reason, otherwise they are at the end of the list of reasons (see Gavin Builds a Sandpit in Chapter 1).

Next comes the summary, covering some of the possible conclusions. Sometimes the conclusions are stated quite generally to help you bring out principles and the philosophical significance of the children's views, e.g., in The Magic Words (Chapter 4) we have categorised reasons for saying thank you into reasons of self-interest, moral reasons and reasons from authority.

Follow up activities are included at the end of each enquiry. You can choose whether or not to use them, and if you use them, you can do so either straight after the enquiry or on another day as an aid to revisiting the topic. In some enquiries alternative versions are provided, to show how the story or props may be varied to suit the interests of different age groups.

Occasionally we suggest a slightly more advanced way to make a philosophical point. The relevant terms or sentences are put in brackets. For instance, in the summary of Beautiful Things (Chapter 5) we put brackets around 'fulfils its function well' as a more advanced way of saying 'does its job well'. You may wish to try out these variations with older children.

Though the enquiry plans give many possible answers, reasons, objections, counterexamples and conclusions, it is important to remember that these are only suggestions, and your enquiry may have gone in a different way and reached different conclusions. What matters is not where you end up, but whether the children can provide reasons for whatever conclusions they have reached.

Using the enquiry plans

As with all teaching it is important to be properly prepared and organised. Before holding a philosophical enquiry with your children you should read the enquiry plan carefully and gather any props you wish to use. Props help to enhance the stories and maintain the interest of the children, and we suggest that you make a collection of suitable resources to be used with the enquiries. If you wish, you can use a philosophy box, which is a large and attractive box, into which you put this book and any necessary props. At the beginning of each session the box is brought out and placed in the middle of the circle in which the children are sitting, which creates a feeling of excitement and anticipation.

Keep the plan with you throughout the enquiry so that you can refer to it. An enquiry usually lasts between 20 and 30 minutes. The children should sit in a circle, usually on the floor. The enquiries will work with a whole class, but it is preferable to use smaller groups of about 10 to 15. It is easier to keep the attention of a smaller group and this allows all the children to make a contribution. Most children will contribute without being asked but some will need a little encouragement. Make sure that you allow the children some thinking time. It is not necessary to demand a response, as you will find that after a few enquiries even the quietest children will gain in confidence and start to contribute. The children should be encouraged to talk directly to each other and not through you.

You are the facilitator of the enquiry and it is your job to keep the discussion focused, but you must be careful not to be too domineering. You have to respect the children's opinions and not put over your own values. As the facilitator you will find that when the children have given a reason you will often need to keep asking questions in order to help them to vocalise their thoughts and to challenge their thinking, which will encourage them to be creative in developing their own ideas.

Start the enquiry by presenting the stimulus, normally a story, and explaining any words that may be unfamiliar to the children. Some initial discussion of the events in the story might occur but this should be kept short, as the main aim is to discuss the philosophical question. Ask the first question on the enquiry plan and encourage the children to give reasons for their answers. We have charts in some enquiries to record their answers and for other enquiries you may find it helpful to write the children's responses on the board as an aid to discussion, both for the children and yourself. Find out who agrees or disagrees with whom. During the enquiry you will find that the children will not always agree with each other, in which case you will need to use all parts of the enquiries – the 'if the children answer yes' part and also the 'if the children answer no' part.

The enquiry plans list some possible answers to questions; some are ones that the children are likely to give, others are ones that we suggest. You can introduce any of these possible answers to encourage discussion. When using the counterexamples and objections, you should ensure that the children know that it is acceptable to change their minds, providing of course that they can give reasons for doing so. It is

Mini Philosophy Helpers used as evaluation cards

also perfectly fine for them to reject the objections or counterexamples, provided that they can explain why they do so. The counterexamples and objections do not cover all possibilities, so you should treat them as suggestions on which you can model your own responses.

You will know when it is time to end the enquiry, for instance, when the children get restless or begin to repeat themselves. It is important to be flexible about the time as even with the same group of children the length of an enquiry can vary a great deal, since some topics will interest them more than others. At the end you should summarise what the children have said, being careful to include everyone's views.

After you have summarised the discussion, you can end by asking the children to evaluate the enquiry. Using happy and sad cards for voting is a fun way to help them to do this. We use Mini Philosophy Helpers; you can use these or devise your own cards. In response to an evaluative question the children hold up the appropriate card.

Examples of questions you can ask are:

- Did you enjoy philosophy today?
- Did you listen well?
- Did you do a lot of thinking?
- Did you talk?

Ask the children to give reasons for their answers so that you can adapt your practice next time if necessary.

A philosophy session in brief
- You and the children sit in a circle on the floor.
- The rules of a philosophy session are recapped using the Philosophy Helpers (when necessary).
- This book and appropriate props are produced (in a philosophy box if you are using one).
- The story is read or the pictures shown or the activity done.

- The question is asked.
- The discussion takes place – with additional questions, objections and counterexamples when appropriate.
- The session is summarised.
- The evaluation cards are used.
- The follow up activity takes place (optional).

Conclusion

Holding a philosophical enquiry is an enjoyable experience for you and the children. It should be an activity that the children look forward to and it will be, if you present it with enthusiasm and create a stimulating atmosphere. We have found that most of the children enjoy philosophy and do so for a variety of reasons, e.g., a four-year-old said, 'I like to ask questions.' and a three-year-old stated, 'I like philosophy because you can think and talk when you are ready to.'

We hope that philosophy will soon become embedded in your classroom practice and that you and your children enjoy using our enquiries.

Chapter 1

Political philosophy

Fairness and rules

THE TEDDY BEARS' PICNIC

Philosophical topic

Political philosophy – fairness: equality versus need.

Aim

To get the children to discuss whether fairness is a matter of equality (equal shares) or distribution according to needs.

Props

- Two small teddies and one large teddy.
- A tablecloth, plates and a cake.

Story

The two small teddies are going to have a picnic. When they have found a shady patch of grass they spread out the tablecloth, set out the plates and put the cake in the centre. 'How shall we share this cake?' asks one teddy. 'Well, let's share it fairly between us', answers the other.

Question

In order to be fair how should the teddies divide the cake between them?

Story (continues)

The teddies decide that it would be fair to share the cake equally. Big Teddy, who is huge, is walking along and sees the picnic. 'Hello, that looks like a delicious cake. Can I join your picnic please and have a piece of the cake?' 'Of course you can', says one of the teddies. Big Teddy sits down and says, 'I should have a bigger piece of cake than you two because I am much bigger and therefore I need more cake than you do.'

Question

Is it fair that Big Teddy has more cake?

If the children answer yes, ask them:
Why is it fair that Big Teddy has more cake?

Possible reasons:

- Big Teddy will be unhappy if he doesn't get more cake. Objection: the two teddies will be unhappy if he does.
- Big Teddy is bigger than the other two teddies, so he needs more food. Since he needs more food, it's fair that he has more. Follow up question: do you think that we should always share things so that people who need more are given more? E.g., if one child has a worse cold than another, he or she needs more tissues, so should be given more.

OR

If the children answer no, ask them:
Why is it not fair that Big Teddy has more cake?

Possible reasons:

- Big Teddy is being greedy. Objection: he's not being greedy, since he needs more food because he's bigger.
- All three teddies ought to have an equal amount of food, since we share things equally with other children. Objection: you are not very different in size but Big Teddy is much bigger than the two teddies and needs more food.
- If Big Teddy gets more cake he will be happy, but the two teddies will be unhappy; and it is better that two teddies are happy than if only one is.
- Things ought always to be shared equally.

Counterexample: you've said that it's not fair that Big Teddy has more cake. At tea-time do mum and dad have more food on their plate? Why is this? Is it because they are bigger and need more food? If so, it must be fair that Big Teddy has more cake than the other two teddies because he is bigger, like your mum and dad are bigger than you, so he needs more. Do you agree now that he should have more cake?

Summary

First, state the question we have discussed: we have been talking about how to share things fairly.
Second, summarise what the children have said. The possibilities include:

- Things should always be shared equally.
- Things should be shared according to need.

Follow up activity

Now divide the cake amongst the children and yourself. Use the principle that the majority of the children have agreed with. Maybe you will be lucky and get a bigger piece of cake than they do!

Alternative version

Twins have a birthday party. The twins take the place of the two small teddies and Jane, a taller friend, takes the part of Big Teddy.

GAVIN BUILDS A SANDPIT

Philosophical topic

Political philosophy – fairness and refusing to help.

Aim

To get the children to discuss whether it is fair not to share if someone has refused to help you, no matter what the reason for the refusal.

Props

- Gavin, John and David (dolls, pictures or cut outs).

Story

Gavin decided to build a sandpit in his garden. His mum said that he could use the stones in the corner of the garden to build the walls and she would buy him some sand. Gavin asked his friend John if he would help him to carry the stones and build the wall. 'No, I'm too busy playing on my skateboard to help you', said John. 'But can I play in your sandpit when you've finished it?' he asked. Gavin replied, 'No, you can't, because you won't help me.' So Gavin moved all the stones by himself and built the walls. He was very tired when he had finished.

Question

Do you think that it was fair that Gavin refused to share his sandpit with John?

If the children answer yes, ask them:
Why do you think it was fair for Gavin to refuse to share his sandpit with John?

Possible reasons:

- John could have helped him but refused to do so.
- Gavin did the work in making the sandpit but John didn't.
- John was being unfriendly in not helping him. Follow up question: is Gavin also being unfriendly in refusing to let John play in the sandpit?
- John was being selfish in not helping, since he wanted to play in the sandpit but didn't want to do the work in making it.

OR

If the children answer no, ask them:
Why do you think it was not fair for Gavin to refuse to share his sandpit with John?

Possible reasons:
- You should always forgive someone, even when they've refused to help you. Follow up question: does whether you should forgive someone depend on how much you needed help? E.g., if Gavin had hurt himself badly and John refused to help, should Gavin forgive John?
- John was his friend, so Gavin should have shared the sandpit with him.

Story (continues)

After having a rest, Gavin went to get the sand that his mum had just brought home. 'I will need someone to help me lift this bag of sand into the sandpit', thought Gavin. Just then he saw his next-door neighbour, David, in his garden and asked him to help with the sand. 'No, I can't help because I have hurt my arm', said David. 'But can I play in your sandpit when you've finished it?' he asked. Gavin replied, 'No you can't, because you won't help me.' Gavin struggled with the bag of sand by himself and managed to fill the sandpit. He then went into the house to collect his bucket and spade, and began to play in the sandpit on his own.

Question

Do you think that it was fair that Gavin refused to share his sandpit with David?

If the children answer yes, ask them:
Why do you think it was fair for Gavin to refuse to share his sandpit with David?

Possible reasons:
- Gavin did the work in making the sandpit but David didn't.
- David was being unfriendly in not helping Gavin.
- David was selfish in not helping Gavin. Objection (also to the reason above): David could not have helped because of his sore arm, so he wasn't being unfriendly or selfish. In contrast, John could have helped Gavin.

OR

If the children answer no, ask them:
Why do you think it was not fair for Gavin to refuse to share his sandpit with David?

Possible reasons:
- You should always forgive someone, even when they've refused to help you.
- David was his friend, so Gavin should have shared the sandpit with him.
- David had a sore arm and couldn't help, so he had a good reason for refusing to help. But John could have helped but chose not to do so. So Gavin should distinguish between the reasons why his friends refused to help him.

Follow up question: I am making bread and I ask you all to help me, but you say that you cannot help because you have sore hands. Is this a good reason why you cannot help? Would it be fair for me not to share the bread with you if this was your reason for not helping me?

Summary

First, state the question we have discussed: we have been talking about whether it is fair not to share if somebody refuses to help you.
Second, summarise what the children have said. The possibilities include:
- It is fair to refuse to share if someone refuses to help you.
- It is not fair to refuse to share, even if someone refuses to help you (i.e., you ought to share with them).
- We should distinguish between the reasons why someone refuses to help. It is fair to refuse to share if someone refuses to help you without a good reason. But if they have a good reason, it is not fair to refuse to share with them (i.e., you ought to share with them).

Follow up activity

Ask the children to think of a reason why they could not help Gavin to build his sandpit. Discuss each reason to decide if it is a good reason to refuse to help Gavin.

THE ANIMAL SNACK

Philosophical topic

Political philosophy – sharing fairly and prudence.

Aim

To get the children to discuss how to share fairly when only one person has been prudent in saving for the future.

Props

- Mole and Rabbit (toys, pictures or cut outs).
- A bag with ten grapes.

Story

Mole and Rabbit are out for a walk when they sit down for a rest. 'Let's have the grapes you have been carrying in your bag', says Mole. 'That's a good idea', says Rabbit. 'Let's have all of the ten grapes just now, so you can have three and I'll have the rest.'

Question

Is this a fair way to share the grapes?

Story (continues)

Mole replies, 'That's not a fair way to share the grapes. I want an equal share. That means I'm going to have five grapes and you can have five grapes.' They share the grapes equally and Rabbit eats all of his very quickly. 'I don't want to eat all my grapes just now', says Mole. 'I may get hungry in a little while, so I'm going to save these two for later.' He puts his two grapes back in the bag. Mole and Rabbit set off on their walk again, through the woods and along beside a river. They decide to stop and paddle in the river. 'I'm hungry again', says Rabbit. 'Let's eat the rest of the grapes and this time I'll share them equally, like you said we should last time.' 'Oh no', says Mole. 'You can't have any. I should have both of the grapes, because I saved them from last time.'

Question

Is it fair that Mole has the two grapes and Rabbit has none?

If the children answer yes, ask them:
Why is it fair that Mole has the two grapes?

Possible reasons:

- He saved them from last time.
- Rabbit and Mole will have had five grapes each, if Mole has the two grapes.
- Rabbit is being greedy. Objection: he isn't being greedy; he's just being fair, since he's dividing things equally.
- Rabbit is selfish because he wanted to divide the grapes unequally the first time, and only wanted to divide them equally when it was in his interest to do so.

OR

If the children answer no, ask them:
Why is it not fair that Mole has the two grapes?

Possible reasons:

- We should always divide things equally, even when someone has had more in the past. Counterexample: suppose that there were 100 grapes and Rabbit had eaten 98: would it still be fair to divide the remaining two grapes equally?
- It would be unkind for Mole to eat the two grapes while Rabbit has to watch and has none.
- Rabbit is hungry and if you're hungry it's fair that you have some more food. Counterexample: you may be hungry but it could still be unfair to take more food, e.g., taking food from your little brother.

Summary

First, state the question we have discussed: we have been talking about how to share things fairly when someone has saved something for later and another person hasn't.
Second, summarise what the children have said. The possibilities include:

- It is always fair to share equally, even when one person hasn't saved and the other one has.
- If one person has saved and the other hasn't, then it's unfair to share equally what has been saved.

Follow up activity

Get the children to finish the story, either by writing it, telling it or by drawing a picture. What does Rabbit say in reply to Mole? Does he get one grape or does Mole get both? How do Rabbit and Mole feel?

Alternative version

Judy and Tom are given £2 each by Granny. Judy saves hers in her piggy bank. Tom spends all of his on a toy car. Next day Tom says to Judy that he wants half of Judy's money to buy another car. Should Judy give half of her money to Tom?

SCHOOL RULES

Philosophical topic

Political philosophy – obeying the rules.

Aim

To get the children to discuss when and why we should obey rules.

Story

We have many rules in our school. (Provide some examples from your school.)

Question

Should we always obey the rules?

If the children answer yes, ask them:

Why should we always obey the rules?

Possible reasons:

- The rules are made to keep us safe, e.g., not running in the corridor. Counterexample: what if in exceptional circumstances the rules don't keep us safe? E.g., if a big dangerous animal escapes in school, we may need to run in the corridor to escape.
- The rules are made so that we can all cooperate with each other.
- The teachers tell us to obey the rules. Counterexample: what if a teacher tells us not to obey a rule? E.g., we have a rule to tidy up at the end of the day. But we haven't finished making a big painting, so the teacher tells us to keep our paints and paper on the floor until the next morning.
- The rules are there to make sure that things go well. Counterexample: what if in exceptional circumstances following the rule would be bad? E.g., we have a rule not to shout. But if we have a visitor who is hard of hearing, he wouldn't hear us if we didn't shout.

OR

If the children answer no, ask them:

Why should we not always obey the rules?

Possible reasons:

- We shouldn't obey the rules, if in exceptional circumstances following the rule would lead to bad things happening (e.g., a big dangerous animal has escaped or there is a hard of hearing visitor – see above).
- We shouldn't obey the rules if a teacher tells us not to obey the rules (e.g., they tell us not to tidy up – see above).
- We shouldn't obey a rule if someone invents a rule that is very silly. For example, a rule that says we have to put up an umbrella every time we go outside even when it's not raining.
- We shouldn't obey a rule if someone who doesn't have the right to invent a rule for our school does so, e.g., someone who has nothing to do with our school.

Summary

First, state the question we have discussed: we have been talking about when and why we should always obey the rules.

Second, summarise what the children have said. The possibilities include:

- We should always obey the rules, e.g., because they keep us safe and allow us to cooperate.
- It is alright not to obey the rules in certain exceptional circumstances, e.g., when following a rule would lead to bad things happening, or when a teacher tells us to ignore a rule.

Follow up activity

Ask the children in pairs to make up two rules, one rule which they consider to be a good rule and one which they consider to be not good or silly. Then get them to discuss their rules with the other children.

Chapter 2

Environmental philosophy

Green land, waste and recycling

GREENHILL VILLAGE

Philosophical topic

Environmental philosophy – use of green land.

Aim

To get the children to discuss whether green land should always be kept green.

Props

- Mr Greene, Mrs Holmes and Mrs Carr (dolls, pictures or cut outs).
- Voting cards: cut outs of a tree, a house and a car, enough for every child to have one of each.
- The story of Greenhill Village, which is at the end of this enquiry.

Story

Read the story.

Activity

Give each child a tree, a house and a car. If they agree to the following questions, the child places the appropriate item in the middle of the circle. Explain to them that they can choose only one option.

- Do you agree with Mr Greene that the land should be kept as green land?
- Do you agree with Mrs Holmes that the land should be used for houses?
- Do you agree with Mrs Carr that the land should be used for a car park?

Get the children to count the number of trees, houses and cars in the middle of the circle.

Question

You've heard the story of Greenhill Village and voted on how the land should be used. Should green land always be kept green?

If the children answer yes, ask them:
Why should green land always be kept green?

Possible reasons:

- The land looks nice.
- The land is home to nice animals and insects. Counterexample: what if the animals are dangerous?
- We can use other land to build houses and car parks on.
- The land can be used to play on.

Counterexample: you've said that green land should always be kept green, but if we had said this in the past, we would not have any houses, or schools or car parks at all.

OR

If the children answer no, ask them:

Why should green land not always be kept green?

Possible reasons:

- We should use it for car parks, since we have lots of cars, so we need somewhere to park them. Objection: what if we should have fewer cars, since they are causing a lot of pollution?
- We need houses for people to live in.
- We need land for school and hospitals.

Follow up question: you've said that green land should sometimes be used for these other purposes. If this is the last piece of green land left, should you use it for other purposes?

Summary

First, state the question we have discussed: we have been talking about whether we should always keep green land green.

Second, summarise what the children have said. The possibilities include:

- It is always wrong to build on green land.
- It is alright to build on green land if we use the land for a basic need, e.g., houses or schools.
- It is alright to build on green land if we use it for something that we want, e.g., to park our cars on.

Follow up activities

Ask the younger children to draw two pictures, one of a farmer in his field and another of shops built on the land. The children should discuss which use of the land they prefer and why.

Ask the older children to role play. You have a large green field at the end of your street. A building company wants to build some shops. Divide your group so that you have representatives for the building company, the owner of the field, and people who live in your street, some of whom agree and some of whom disagree with the proposal. Ask one person from each group to make a short statement about why the land should be used in a certain way. Then get them to discuss their reasons with each other. See if they can come to a conclusion about how the land should be used.

The story: Greenhill Village

The village of Greenhill was surrounded by beautiful countryside. There were lots of fields, trees and wild flowers. But the villagers disagreed about how to use this green land.

Mr Greene thought that it should be kept as green land and nothing should be built on it.

Mrs Holmes wanted to use the land to build houses. She said, 'There are people who are homeless and if we built houses, these people would have somewhere to live.'

Mrs Carr thought that the land should be used to build a car park. She said, 'We don't have enough space to park our cars, so we will build a car park.'

The villagers held a meeting to decide what it would be best to do.

EMERALD THE ELEPHANT

Philosophical topic

Environmental philosophy – wasting water.

Aim

To get the children to discuss whether it is always wrong to waste water.

Props

- An elephant, a tiger and a lion (toys, pictures or cut outs).
- The story of Emerald the Elephant, which is at the end of this enquiry.

Story

Read the story.

Question

Do you think that it was wrong for Emerald to waste the water?

If the children answer yes, ask them:

Why do you think it was wrong for Emerald to waste the water?

Possible reasons:

- There was no water left to drink.
- There was no water left to wash in.
- There was no water left to play in.
- No water was left for the plants.
- Emerald was being selfish not to leave some water for other animals.

OR

If the children answer no, ask them:

Why do you think it was not wrong for Emerald to waste the water?

Possible reasons:

- Emerald was having fun and playing.
- More water will fill the lake the next time it rains.
- There is plenty of water left elsewhere.

Question

Is it always wrong to waste water?

If the children answer yes, ask them:
Why is it always wrong to waste water?

Possible reasons:

- We might run out of water.
- We need to drink water to stay alive.
- We need water to clean things and flush the toilet.

Counterexamples: you've said that it's always wrong to waste water, but think about the following:

- If the water coming out of the tap is dirty, shouldn't you leave the tap running until the water runs clear?
- Suppose that it rains a lot, so whenever we use water there is always some more left. What's wrong with wasting water then?

Follow up question: what's the difference between these two cases and the story where Emerald wastes water?

Possible answer:

- The water in Emerald's lake is clean and there's only a limited supply of it, whereas in the counterexamples, the water is dirty or there is an unlimited supply of it.

OR

If the children answer no, ask them:
Why is it not always wrong to waste water?

Possible reasons:

- The rain will bring more water.
- Sometimes there is an unlimited supply of water.
- Sometimes water is dirty and can make you sick, so we have to get rid of it.

Follow up question: suppose there is only a limited supply of water and it's clean. Isn't it wrong to waste the water then?

Summary

First, state the question we have discussed: we have been talking about whether it is always wrong to waste water.

Second, summarise what the children have said. The possibilities include:

- It's always wrong to waste water.
- It's not always wrong to waste water, since the water may be dirty or there may be an unlimited supply of it.

Follow up activity

Get the children to draw a picture of someone wasting water. Ask them to show their pictures to the group and ask the group to discuss whether it shows a situation in which it is wrong to waste water or not.

Alternative version

Martin and Spot, his dog, are playing in the paddling pool. They splash so much that no water is left. When Martin's big brother, Michael, comes home from school he is upset because he wanted to cool down and also play in the water.

The story: Emerald the Elephant

Emerald the elephant was walking through the jungle feeling very hot when she saw a small lake. The water in the lake was lovely and very clean, so she could drink it and play in it. Emerald ran into the water splashing with her big feet and squirting water through her trunk, trying to hit the trees around the lake. She spent a long time playing, and only stopped when there was no water left in the lake. 'I'll have to stop playing and go and find something else to do', she said.

As Emerald turned away from the lake she saw her friends Larch, a lion, and Titus, a tiger, running towards the lake. 'I'm really thirsty. I'll be able to get a big drink in the lake', Larch was shouting. 'My fur is dirty from playing in all that mud. I need to wash before I go home', said Titus. When they reached the lake they stopped and stared. 'Where has all the water gone?' said Titus. 'I don't know. There was plenty here yesterday', replied Larch. They looked around and saw Emerald. 'Do you know where the water has gone?' asked Larch. 'I was playing and squirted all the water at the trees', said Emerald. 'You wasted all that water when we needed it to drink and to wash in', said Titus. 'I'm sorry. I was having such fun playing I didn't think about how much water I was using', apologised Emerald. 'Well we'll just have to go and find some water elsewhere, since it's not going to rain for a long time, so the lake won't fill up again soon', said Larch, and off they went back through the trees, leaving Emerald on her own. Emerald felt very sorry because she had not thought about how she was wasting water.

BENNY THE BIN

Philosophical topic

Environmental philosophy – recycling.

Aim

To get the children to discuss whether and why we should recycle.

Story

Mrs Green went outside her back door with a bag full of rubbish. 'I must recycle all this rubbish and put it into the correct bins', she said to herself. She put the newspapers in the paper bin, the plastic bottles in the bin for plastic, and the glass in the bin for glass. Feeling very pleased with herself she turned to go back into the house, but stopped when she heard a voice. 'I'm fed up with having all this disgusting rubbish put into me', the voice said. Mrs Green was astonished: it was one of the bins speaking. 'Who are you?' she asked. 'I'm Benny', replied the bin. 'What should I do with my rubbish, if you don't want it?' asked Mrs Green. 'Well', said Benny, 'just throw all the rubbish into the garden.' 'Oh no, I couldn't do that', said Mrs Green. 'It's very important that I recycle all my rubbish.' 'No it's not!' said Benny. 'It would be much quicker for you just to throw all of your rubbish into one pile in the garden. Only you will see the mess and it will soon rot away.'

Question

Benny says that Mrs Green ought to throw all of her rubbish into her garden. Do you think that his reasons are good ones?

If the children answer yes, ask them:

Why do you think that Benny's reasons are good ones?

Possible answers:

- He's correct that it's quicker and easier just to dump all the rubbish in the garden, rather than sort it into different bins, so it's alright to do so. Counterexample: sometimes it's easier to do something that is wrong, e.g., it's easier not to tidy your room than to tidy it.

- It's Mrs Green's garden, so if she wanted to dump the rubbish into her garden, it's alright for her to do so.
- The paper will rot away so the garden will soon be tidy again. Objection: the glass and plastic won't rot away.

OR

If the children answer no, ask them:
Why do you think that Benny's reasons are not good ones?

Possible answers:

- If we always sort our rubbish, we will get fast at it.
- Mrs Green's neighbours will see the mess too.
- Mrs Green may not want a mess in her garden.
- Some of the rubbish (the plastic and glass) won't rot away and will stay forever in her garden.

Story (continues)

'Oh, I couldn't just throw my rubbish into the garden', said Mrs Green. 'You have to recycle, because the rubbish can be made into other things. The rubbish would also look horrible and stop me growing my vegetables.'

Question

Mrs Green says that she ought not to throw away her rubbish into her garden, but should recycle it. Do you think that her reasons are good ones?

If the children answer yes, ask them:
Why do you think that Mrs Green's reasons are good ones?

Possible answers:

- It's wasteful to throw away things that we could use again.
- If we don't dump rubbish in the garden, we can use the garden for useful things like growing food or playing in.
- Rubbish looks horrible. Counterexample: some rubbish looks nice, e.g., a colourful chair.
- It is Mrs Green's garden, so if she doesn't want to dump rubbish in it, that is alright.

OR

If the children answer no, ask them:
Why do you think Mrs Green's reasons are not good ones?

Possible answers:

- The newspapers would rot away, so her garden would in the end look nice again and she could grow her vegetables. Objection: the glass and the plastic won't rot away.

- Some rubbish can't be recycled, so can't be used again, e.g., nappies and light bulbs.
- Some rubbish may be pretty, e.g., a glass vase. Objection: most rubbish looks and smells horrible.

Summary

First, state the question we have discussed: we have been talking about whether and why we should recycle.

Second, summarise what the children have said. The possibilities include:
- We should recycle because it avoids waste, since we can use things again; it keeps land free from rubbish so that we can use it for good things like growing food; and some rubbish will never rot away but can be recycled.
- We shouldn't recycle because it requires more effort and time; some people don't mind dumping rubbish on their own land; and some rubbish will rot away on its own.

Follow up activity

Bring a box of rubbish and ask the children to discuss which things can be recycled and which things cannot.

Chapter 3

Social philosophy

Friends and relationships

TEDDY'S FRIENDS

Philosophical topic

Social philosophy – characteristics of a good friend.

Aim

To get the children to discuss what makes someone a good friend.

Props

- A chart (heading: How to be friendly).
- Several teddies: Theodore and one teddy for each child.

Story

This is Theodore's first day at school. He has been brought into the classroom and his mum has just left him.

Question

How do you think Theodore is feeling?

Possible answers:

- Frightened.
- Nervous.
- Lonely.
- Excited.
- Happy.

Story (continues)

We have lots of teddies here who are all friends with each other. (Give one teddy to each child.)

Question

What could each teddy do to show that he would like to be friends with Theodore? List the children's answers on the chart.

Possible answers:
- Show Theodore around the classroom.
- Ask him to play with them.
- Talk to Theodore.
- Tell him their names.
- Hold his hand.
- Share crayons with him.
- Help him fasten his coat.

Discuss the suggestions on the chart. If the children agree that the suggestion would make a person a good friend, they should hold up their teddy and give their reasons.

Question

Can you think of ways to group these answers together to show what makes someone a good friend?

Possible groups:
- Doing things together, e.g., playing together.
- Sharing things, e.g., crayons.
- Being affectionate towards each other, e.g., holding their hand.
- Helping each other, e.g., helping put on coats.

Summary

First, state the question we have discussed: we have been talking about what makes someone a good friend.

Second, summarise what the children have decided. The possibilities include:
- Good friends do things together.
- Good friends share things.
- Good friends are nice to each other.
- Good friends help each other.

Follow up activity

Ask the children to sort the following statements into those that show the person would make a good friend and those that do not, and to discuss their reasons. These can be presented as printed cards for the older children to sort by themselves.
- Susan asked John if he would like to play football with her.
- Mary and Jane took the dog for a walk together.
- David told Jim that he would not let him ride his bike.
- Jenny helped Mary find a book she needed for her homework.
- Scott walked away from Susan when she fell over and hurt her knee.
- James went over to talk to David who was sitting on his own.

WILLIAM AND ARTHUR

Philosophical topic

Social philosophy – friendship and sharing.

Aim

To get the children to discuss whether we should share everything with our friends.

Props

• The story of William and Arthur, which is at the end of this enquiry.

Story

Read the story.

Question

When did William and Arthur stop being friends?

Answer:

When they stopped sharing the football and the books.

Question

Should you share everything with your friends?

If the children answer yes, ask them:

Why should you share everything with your friends?

Possible reasons:

• By sharing we show we care about our friends.
• We feel good when we share with our friends.
• If we share, then our friends will share with us.
• We can do some things with our friends only if we share, e.g., playing football.

Counterexample: you've said that you should share everything with your friends, but what if you have a cold – should you share it with a friend?

Follow up question to the counterexample: what should you not share with your friends?

Possible answers:

- Anything that is bad, e.g., a cold.
- Your name: it would be confusing if everyone had exactly the same name.
- Your mum: she is special to you.

OR

If the children answer no, ask them:
Why should you not share everything with your friends?

Possible reasons:

- You can be friends without sharing.
- Sometimes it is nice to keep things for yourself. Objection: isn't sometimes keeping things for yourself selfish?
- You shouldn't share bad things with your friends.
- Some things are special to you, e.g., your mum.

Summary

First, state the question we have discussed: we have been talking about whether we should share everything with our friends.
Second, summarise what the children have said. The possibilities include:

- We should share everything with our friends.
- We should share only good things with our friends.
- It is not alright to share things that are really special to us, e.g., our mum.

Follow up activity

Ask the children to write about or draw two things that they would like to share with friends, and one thing that they would not like to share. Ask them to discuss their reasons with the group.

The story: William and Arthur

William and Arthur are friends. One day they were in William's garden. 'I'm not going to let you play with my football today', William told Arthur. Arthur was very surprised. 'If you don't share your football with me then we can't play football together and I'm going', replied Arthur. He ran home, leaving William with nobody to play football.

The next day at school William apologised to Arthur and they sat together in the classroom. They needed to share the books but Arthur wanted to use them first. 'You can have them when I'm finished', he told William. 'But I need to get this work finished now', complained William. William was cross with Arthur because he was late getting his work finished and the teacher was not pleased with him. William refused to talk to Arthur at playtime.

When it was time to go home, William and Arthur decided that they had been silly and they should be friends. 'We will share things with each other from now on, as that's what friends do', said William. Arthur agreed with him.

EMMA AND SALLY

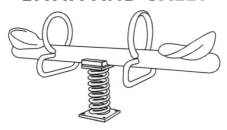

Philosophical topic

Social philosophy – cooperation.

Aim

To get the children to discuss when it is good to cooperate with others.

Props

- Emma and Sally (dolls, pictures or cut outs).
- The story of Emma and Sally, which is at the end of this enquiry.

Story

Read the story.

Question

Emma and Sally cooperated (worked together) in tidying Sally's bedroom, but Sally refused to cooperate with Emma on the seesaw and in crossing the road without her mum. Do you think that it is always good to cooperate with others?

If the children answer yes, ask them:

Why is it always good to cooperate?

Possible reasons:

- Jobs get finished quicker, e.g., Sally's room is tidied quicker.
- It is enjoyable to cooperate with others. Counterexample: sometimes it's not enjoyable, e.g., because you're too tired (like Sally on the seesaw) or you don't like the other person.
- It is kind or helpful or considerate to cooperate with others. Counterexample: what if someone asks you to help them to do something that is wrong, e.g., crossing the road without mum, or stealing?
- If you cooperate with others, they are likely to help you when you need help.

OR

If the children answer no, ask them:

Why is it not always good to cooperate?

Possible reasons:

- When you are being asked to do something that is unkind or selfish or wrong, e.g., Sally refuses to cross the road with Emma because it would be wrong to do so without her mum.
- When you don't want to cooperate, e.g., because you're too tired. Counterexample: what if the other person is doing something that is really important?
- When you are asked to do something you know that you do not have the ability to do properly, because it is so hard.

Summary

First, state the question we have discussed: we have been talking about whether it is always good to cooperate with others.

Second, summarise what the children have said. The possibilities include:

- It is always good to cooperate, e.g., because it is kind, or enjoyable or in your interests.
- It is not always good to cooperate, e.g., when you are being asked to do something wrong, or to do something you know that you cannot do properly.

Follow up activity

Ask the children in groups to write a list of situations when it would be good to cooperate with other children in the classroom and when it would not be good to cooperate. Get the children to compare their lists with the other groups and discuss their reasons.

The story: Emma and Sally

Emma arrives at Sally's door. 'Can you come and play with me?' she asks Sally. 'I can't come out until I've tidied my bedroom', says Sally. 'OK, shall we tidy it together because that way it will be done much quicker and then we will have longer to play?' asks Emma. 'That's a good idea', replies Sally. They both go into Sally's bedroom and the mess is soon tidied up. 'That was fun tidying together', says Sally. Sally's mum then takes the girls across the road to play in the park. 'I will be back for you in half an hour. Wait for me and do not cross the road by yourselves', she tells them.

'Come and play on the seesaw, because I can't make it go up and down on my own', says Emma. 'No I don't want to, I'm too tired', says Sally. Sally goes and sits on the bench to have a rest while Emma sits on the seesaw feeling very unhappy.

Emma then decides she wants to go home. 'Let's go now, I want to go home. We will be safe crossing the road together.' 'No, we have to wait until my mum comes for us', says Sally. Emma starts to cry, 'I want to go now, please let's cross the road together.' 'No', says Sally. Just then the girls see Sally's mum coming into the park. 'I'm pleased you waited for me', she says. They all cross the road together.

MAISIE THE SHEEP

Philosophical topic

Social philosophy – being different from others.

Aim

To get the children to discuss whether it is good to be different from other people.

Props

• The story of Maisie the Sheep, which is at the end of this enquiry.

Story

Read Part 1 of the story.

Question

Is it always good to be different, or never good to be different, or sometimes good to be different from other people?

If the children answer that it is always good to be different, ask them:

Why is it always good to be different from other people?

Possible reasons:

• It is nice to be yourself and not like everybody else. Objection: you will not be like everyone else, even if you are only sometimes different from them.
• You may be different because you can do things that others can't.
• People may praise and admire you for being different.

Counterexample: you've said that it's always good to be different. Now listen to another story about Maisie. (Read Part 2 of the story.) On the second day, Maisie is different from the other sheep, but she is being nasty to them. Is it still good for Maisie to be different?

OR

If the children answer that it is never good to be different, ask them:
Why is it never good to be different from other people?

Possible reasons:

- You can't join in with what the group is doing if you are different.
- You don't feel that you belong to the group if you are different.
- People might laugh at you if you are different.

Counterexamples: you've said that it's never good to be different. But think about the following:

- On the first day (Part 1), Maisie is different from the other sheep, because she is eating more, and she can dance and hit the ball; isn't it good in this case for Maisie to be different?
- If we were all exactly the same, looked the same, said the same things, had the same thoughts and the same names, what would it be like then? Would it be good then to be different? So is it good to be different in some ways?

OR

If the children answer that it is sometimes good to be different, ask them:
Why is it sometimes good to be different from other people?

Possible reasons:

- It's good to be different when you can do something better than other people, e.g., Maisie can dance and hit the ball.
- It's good to be different provided that you are not harming anyone else.
- It's not good to be different when you will be laughed at or hurt because you're different. Objection: shouldn't you just ignore them or tell the teacher if they're being unkind?
- It's not good to be different when you're doing something wrong and everyone else is doing something right; e.g., you're making mistakes in maths or being naughty.

Summary

First, state the question we have discussed: we have been talking about whether it is good to be different from other people.
Second, summarise what the children have said. The possibilities include:

- It is always good to be different from others, e.g., because it is nice not to be like everyone else.
- It is never good to be different from others, e.g., because you may get laughed at.
- It is sometimes good to be different from others, e.g., when you can do something better than they can.

Follow up activity

Ask the children to make drawings where a person is doing something different from the others in the picture and it's good, and drawings where a person is doing something different from the others and it's not good. They should explain to the other children why the situations are different.

The story: Maisie the Sheep

Part 1

All the sheep on Farmer Des's farm were the same, except for Maisie. Maisie was different. One day she was quietly eating grass in the corner of the field on her own. The other sheep were all together trying to eat the turnips that the farmer had brought them. 'I'm getting much more to eat than they are', thought Maisie to herself. Later Maisie played with some of the other sheep. They were using the bat and ball. Maisie was the only sheep that could hit the ball. 'I like being the only one that can do something', thought Maisie to herself. At the end of the day Maisie was dancing in the field, kicking her legs high. The other sheep came to watch. 'Sheep don't dance', they told her. But Maisie was enjoying herself and didn't want to stop.

Part 2

The next day Maisie was quietly eating grass in the corner of the field on her own, because she had shouted at the other sheep and told them they could not have any of the grass. Later Maisie played with some of the other sheep. They were using the bat and ball. Maisie was the only sheep that could hit the ball. She was hitting the ball at the other sheep to hurt them. At the end of the day Maisie was dancing in the field, kicking her legs high. The other sheep came to watch. 'Sheep don't dance', they told her. But Maisie wasn't really dancing; she was trying to kick the other sheep.

BIG TEDDY'S NEW SCHOOL

Philosophical topic

Social philosophy – inclusion.

Aim

To get the children to discuss whether they should always include others in the group.

Props

• A big teddy and four smaller teddies.

Story

Big Teddy has moved to a new town and this is his first day at his new school. When he comes into the classroom he looks around and sees the other teddies are all busy. Some are writing, some are painting and some are playing. He looks at two teddies who are making things with building blocks. Big Teddy has lots of building blocks at home and he loves building things. He asks the two teddies, 'Can I play with you?' They look up at him and say, 'No.'

Question

Why do you think that these two teddies said that Big Teddy could not play with them?

Possible reasons:

• There is not enough room for more teddies to play.
• There are not enough building blocks for more teddies to play.
• They do not like him.
• They are not kind.

Story (continues)

Big Teddy walks away from the building blocks and wanders around the classroom. He sees another two teddies playing in the house. 'Perhaps they will let me play with them', he thinks. He knocks on the door of the house and when one of the teddies opens the door Big Teddy asks, 'Can I come in and play with you?' 'Of course you can. Have you come to be in our class?' the teddy asks him. 'Yes. This is my first day here', says Big Teddy as he happily goes into the house.

Question

Why do you think that these two teddies said that Big Teddy could play with them?

Possible reasons:

- They need him to play their game.
- They like him.
- They feel sorry for him.
- They are kind.

Question

The first two teddies did not include Big Teddy in their group and the second two teddies did. Should you include everyone all of the time in your group?

If the children answer yes, ask them:
Why should you include everyone all of the time?

Possible reasons:

- It makes everyone happy.
- It stops people from getting upset. Counterexample (also to the reason above): suppose someone in the group would be upset if you included a new person: does that mean that you shouldn't include the new person?
- It is important to be kind to others.

Counterexample: you've said that we should include everyone all of the time, but what if someone is being horrible to other children?

OR

If the children answer no, ask them:
Why should you not include everyone all of the time?

Possible reasons:

- You shouldn't include someone if they are being horrible. Objection: perhaps if you included them, they would stop being horrible.
- It's alright not to include someone if you don't like them. Objection: suppose that no one likes you, do you think that this is a reason why you should be excluded?
- It's alright not to include someone if it would spoil the game because there would be too many people or not enough space.
- It's alright not to include someone if there are not enough toys for everyone to play with.

Summary

First, state the question we have discussed: we have been talking about whether we should always include others in the group.

Second, summarise what the children have said. The possibilities include:
- We should always include others, because it's kind to do so.
- Sometimes we can exclude others when there is a good reason for doing so, e.g., because there is not enough space for them to play.

Follow up activity

Have an Inclusion Day. Ask the children to focus on including others in their classroom activities and outside in the playground. At the end of the day discuss how the children felt about including others and being included themselves. Ask them how easy or difficult this was to do and why this was so.

Chapter 4

Ethics

Virtues and vices

SAM'S KIND DAY

Philosophical topic

Ethics – kindness.

Aim

To get the children to discuss what it means to be kind and whether we should always be kind to others.

Props

- A chart (heading: What can Sam do to be kind?).

Story

Sam was talking with his mum. She asked him, 'What will you do today?' 'I'm going to have a Kind Day when I go around being kind to everyone', he replied. 'What a good idea. What will you do to be kind?' Sam's mum asked.

Activity

Ask the children to suggest things that Sam could do to be kind. Record their answers on the chart.

Question

Referring to the chart, ask the children: what makes these things kind?

Possible answers:
- Sam is looking after others.
- Sam is sharing things with others.
- Sam is giving things to others.
- Sam is helping others. Counterexample (also applies to all of the above): what if the only reason that Sam is doing this is that he expects to get something good back for himself? Is he still kind?
- Sam is helping others, even though he doesn't expect anything good in return for himself.

Question

We've talked about how Sam can be kind. Should we always be kind to others?

If the children answer yes, ask them:
Why should we always be kind to others?

Possible reasons:

- If we are kind to others, they will be kind to us. Objection: if the only reason that you are being kind to someone is that you expect them to be kind to you in return, are you really being kind?
- We will make other people happy.
- It is the right thing to do.
- Adults tell us always to be kind.

Counterexample: you've said that we should always be kind to others, but suppose someone is being nasty to you. Should you still be kind to them?

OR

If the children answer no, ask them:
Why should we sometimes not be kind to others?

Possible reasons:

- We do not need to be kind to other people if they are not kind to us.
- We should not be kind to someone if they have done something very bad.
- Sometimes being kind would stop us from doing something we really want to do. Objection: isn't that just being selfish?

Summary

First, state the question we have discussed: we have been talking about what it means to be kind and whether we should always be kind to others.
Second, summarise what the children have said.
The possibilities about the meaning of kindness include:

- We are kind when we help others.
- We are kind when we help others, even though we do not expect anything good back in return.

The possibilities about whether we should always be kind include:

- We should always be kind to others, e.g., because we will make them happy.
- We should sometimes not be kind to others, e.g., because they have done something wrong, or been nasty to us.

Follow up activity

Ask the children in pairs to make a list of four activities that they consider to be kind and one activity that they consider not to be kind. Read these lists out to the other children and ask them to find the odd one out, the one that is not kind.

KIRSTY

Philosophical topic

Ethics – telling the truth.

Aim

To get the children to discuss whether they should always tell the truth.

Props

- Kirsty (a doll, a picture or a cut out figure).
- The picture of the hat made by Kirsty's granny, which is at the end of this enquiry.

Story

Kirsty's mum asked her if she had moved her toys from the back doorstep. 'Yes, of course I have', replied Kirsty. But she knew that she had not moved them and that her doll and a car were still on the doorstep. 'Good girl', said her mum. 'Now because you have tidied up we can read a story together.' They both sat on the sofa and mum started to read. When mum looked up from the book she saw that it was raining. 'Quick, the washing is out and is getting wet', she exclaimed. She ran through the kitchen, opened the back door and tripped over Kirsty's doll and car. She landed with a bump. When she tried to stand up she discovered that she had hurt her ankle.

Question

Do you think Kirsty should have told her mum the truth?
Ask the children to give reasons for their answers.

Story (continues)

Kirsty's granny was coming to visit. Kirsty loved her granny and always had lots of fun with her. When granny arrived she told Kirsty that she had a present for her. Kirsty was very excited. Granny brought out of her bag a hat. 'I made this hat especially for you', granny told Kirsty. Kirsty took one look at the hat and thought, 'This is an awful hat. I don't like it at all and I can never wear it.' But she said to granny, 'This is a lovely hat. I like it a lot and I'll wear it when I go to school.' Granny smiled and said, 'I'm really pleased you like it. It took me a long time to find the pieces of material to make it for you.'

Question

Do you think that Kirsty should have told her granny the truth?
Ask the children to give reasons for their answers.

Question

If any of the children have said that Kirsty should tell the truth to her mum but not to her granny, ask them the following question. Why do you think that Kirsty should tell the truth to her mum but not to her granny?

Question

We've talked about whether Kirsty should tell the truth to her mum and her granny. Thinking about this, should we always tell the truth?

If the children answer yes, ask them:
Why should we always tell the truth?

Possible reasons:

- It is wrong not to tell the truth.
- We will feel guilty if we do not tell the truth.
- Our parents tell us to always tell the truth.
- We will get into trouble if we do not tell the truth. Counterexample: suppose that no one knew you were not telling the truth, so you wouldn't get into trouble. Would it be alright then not to tell the truth?
- We will harm others if we do not tell the truth. Counterexample: sometimes it harms someone if we do tell the truth, e.g., Kirsty's granny would be upset if Kirsty told her the truth.

OR

If the children answer no, ask them:
Why should we not always tell the truth?

Possible reasons:

- We should not tell the truth if by telling the truth we would not get something we want, e.g., Kirsty wants her mum to read the story. Objections: isn't it dishonest not to tell the truth? How would you like it if people did not tell the truth to you?
- We should not tell the truth when doing so would hurt the feelings of other people.

- We should not tell the truth if not telling the truth makes other people happy. Counterexample: what if the other person would prefer to know the truth rather than be happy?
- We should not tell the truth when someone has told us not to tell the truth. Counterexample: what if this person has done something wrong and doesn't want to be found out?

Summary

First, state the question we have discussed: we have been talking about whether we should always tell the truth.

Second, summarise what the children have said. The possibilities include:

- You must always tell the truth.
- Sometimes it is alright not to tell the truth, for instance, when we do not want to hurt the feelings of others.

Follow up activity

Ask the children to draw a hat that they think Kirsty would have liked. Would she have been able to tell the truth if granny had given her the hats they have drawn? What would she have said?

The hat made by Kirsty's granny

THE MAGIC WORDS

Philosophical topic

Ethics – saying thank you.

Aim

To get the children to discuss when and why you should say thank you.

Props

- The story of The Magic Words, which is at the end of this enquiry.
- A chart (heading: When we say thank you).

Story

Read the story.

Activity

The wizard listened to when the children were saying thank you. Ask the children when they would say thank you. Record their answers on the chart.

Question

Should you always say thank you, or never say thank you, or sometimes say thank you?

If the children answer that you should always say thank you, use these counterexamples:

- Should you say thank you even if no one has given you anything?
- Should you say thank you if someone has refused to give you what you asked for?

OR

If the children answer that you should never say thank you, use this counterexample:

- If someone gives you something really nice that you've asked for, isn't it rude not to thank them?

OR

If the children answer that you should sometimes say thank you, ask them:

When are the times that you should say thank you?

Possible answers:

- When someone gives you something. Counterexample: what if someone is nasty to you, e.g., they hit you and give you a bruise?
- When someone gives you something and they are being nice to you.
- If someone gives you several things one after another, you only have to thank them once, not for each one.

Question

Why should you say thank you?

Possible reasons:

- You won't get what you want, if you don't say thank you. Counterexample: suppose you will get what you want, even if you don't say thank you. Is it alright not to thank the person then?
- People don't like it when you forget to say thank you.
- Mum tells us to say thank you.
- Saying thank you shows that you are a nice person.
- You are polite if you say thank you, and this shows respect to the other person.
- It's wrong not to say thank you. Follow up question: why is it wrong?

Summary

First, state the question we have discussed: we have been talking about when and why you should say thank you.
Second, summarise what the children have said.
The possibilities for when you should say thank you include:
- You should always say thank you.
- You should never say thank you.
- You should say thank you sometimes: for instance, when someone has given you something and they are being nice to you.
The possibilities for why you should say thank you include:
- Reasons of self-interest, e.g., by saying thank you, you are more likely to get what you want.
- Moral reasons, e.g., we ought to be polite because it shows respect.
- Reasons from authority, e.g., doing what your mum tells you to do.

Follow up activity

Prepare materials to make badges: cardboard, and safety pins or sticky labels. Give the material to the children only when they use the magic words. Ask them to use the material to make badges that say: I am a philosopher.

The story: The Magic Words

The wizard took his book of magic spells down from the shelf. 'What magic will I do today?' he thought. After searching through the pages he found a spell for magic words. 'Now all I have to do is to decide what the magic words will be. I think the words "thank you" would be good', he said to himself.

The wizard took spoonfuls of powder from his various bottles and mixed them in his magic pot while reading out the spell from his book.

'Now I will take this potion to [insert the name of your school] and sprinkle it in each of the classrooms and that will make all the children remember to say thank you', the wizard said.

When he had finished, the wizard sat and listened to when the children were saying thank you. He was so pleased that his spell was working and the children were saying the magic words lots of times during the day.

TEDDY SCROOGE

Philosophical topic

Ethics – giving presents.

Aim

To get the children to discuss whether it is alright (permissible) not to give a present back when you have received one.

Props

- Six presents (wrapped empty boxes).
- Three teddies: Teddy Scrooge, Tim and Bob.

Story

The teddies have brought two presents each to give to their friends. Bob gives his presents first. He gives one to Tim and one to Teddy Scrooge. Then Tim gives his presents, one to Bob and one to Teddy Scrooge. But when it is time for Teddy Scrooge to give his presents he says 'I don't want to give my presents away. They are really nice presents. I want to keep them for myself.' Tim and Bob look very surprised. 'But we have given you a present', says Bob. Teddy Scrooge defends himself. 'If you gave me these presents only because you wanted a present back, then they are not really presents.'

Question

Do you think that it is alright that Teddy Scrooge keeps the presents and doesn't give them to Tim and Bob?

If the children answer yes, ask them:

Why is it alright that Teddy Scrooge keeps the presents for himself?

Possible reasons:

- He likes the presents.
- If he doesn't want to give the presents, then he shouldn't have to. Counterexample: we sometimes ought to do what we don't want to do, e.g., tidying our bedrooms.

- A present is something that we give without expecting anything back in return, as Teddy Scrooge says. It's different from buying something, when we expect something back.
- Just because he has been given presents doesn't mean he has to give a present back. Counterexample: if Teddy Scrooge receives presents repeatedly and never gives any presents in return, isn't he being selfish?

OR

If the children answer no, ask them:
Why is it not alright that Teddy Scrooge keeps the presents for himself?

Possible reasons:
- If you are given a present, you should give one back. Counterexample: if you go to a birthday party, you take a present but you do not expect to get a present back.
- He is being selfish, ungrateful and greedy by keeping the presents.
- He is not being a friend to Tim and Bob, since friends care for each other and he is not being caring to them.

Summary

First, state the question we have discussed: we have been talking about whether it is alright (permissible) not to give a present in return when you have received one. Second, summarise what the children have said. The possibilities include:
- It is alright to receive a present and not to give one back, e.g., because it's not really a present if it's been given only to get something back.
- It's not alright to receive a present and not give one back, e.g., because not giving one back is selfish, unfriendly or ungrateful.

Follow up activity

Ask the children in groups to list those occasions when they would give presents without expecting one back, and those occasions when they would be annoyed if they did not get one back. Ask them to discuss the differences between these two sorts of cases.

THE SELFISH HIPPO

Philosophical topic

Ethics – selfishness.

Aim

To get the children to discuss the meaning of selfishness and whether it is wrong to be selfish.

Props

- The story of The Selfish Hippo, which is at the end of this enquiry.

Story

Read the story.

Question

In what ways was Harry selfish?

Answers:

- He wanted the pool to himself and wouldn't share with the other hippos.
- He wouldn't help the monkey in case he hurt himself.
- He ate most of the food himself.

Question

The story is called The Selfish Hippo. What does it mean to be selfish?

Possible answers:

- You don't share things.
- You don't help others. Counterexample (also for the answer above): suppose I help you (or share things with you) only because I'm expecting you to give me something nice in return. Am I not still selfish?
- You are selfish if you don't share things or help others unless doing so is in your own interest.
- You care only for yourself and nobody else.

Question

Is it wrong to be selfish?

If the children answer yes, ask them:

Why is it wrong to be selfish?

Possible reasons:

- We should value everybody.
- We would not be nice people if we were selfish.
- We get pleasure from helping others.
- Nobody would help us when we needed help if we were selfish. Objection: if we are helping only to get help from others, isn't this another kind of selfishness?
- We would have no friends.

OR

If the children answer no, ask them:

Why is it not wrong to be selfish?

Possible reasons:

- Sometimes you have to put yourself first so that you achieve something that is important to you. Counterexample: it may be important to you, but is it really important, e.g., watching your favourite television programme?
- You have to keep some things for yourself and not share them, e.g., you should not share your maths answers.
- Other people are selfish, so why shouldn't you be selfish as well? Objection: if someone is doing something wrong, that doesn't mean that it is alright for you to do something wrong as well.

Summary

First, state the question we have discussed: we have been talking about the meaning of selfishness and whether it is wrong to be selfish.
Second, summarise what the children have said.
The possibilities about the meaning of selfishness include:

- You are selfish if you don't share things or help others unless doing so is in your interest.
- You are selfish if you don't care about anyone else.

The possibilities about whether it is wrong to be selfish include:

- It is wrong to be selfish, because we ought to value everyone.
- It is not wrong to be selfish, if being selfish is the only way to get important things done.

Follow up activity

Ask the children in pairs to make either a single picture of someone being selfish, or a short comic strip of four pictures to show a situation in which someone is selfish and the consequences of this. Each pair of children should discuss their pictures with another pair.

The story: The Selfish Hippo

One very hot day Harry the hippo was cooling off in a pool. Three hippos came down to join him. 'You're not getting in here with me, because there wouldn't be enough space for me', shouted Harry. 'Of course there's enough room. But we'll just go somewhere else and leave you on your own', replied one of the other hippos.

Later Harry went to find his friends. On his way he saw a monkey who had his hand stuck under a fallen tree. 'Harry, can you move this tree for me?' asked the monkey. 'No, I would hurt myself climbing through all these fallen trees', answered Harry and walked past.

When Harry found his friends they were eating. 'Can I have some?' he asked. 'Yes', they said. Harry took most of the food for himself. 'You must leave some of the food for the rest of us', said one of his friends. 'No, I want it all to myself', answered Harry. He ate most of the food himself and then left his friends.

CHARLOTTE THE LAZY CATERPILLAR

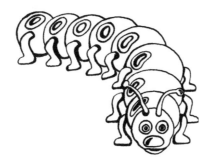

Philosophical topic

Ethics – laziness.

Aim

To get the children to discuss whether it is wrong to be lazy, either when you harm only yourself or when you harm someone else.

Story

Charlotte the lazy caterpillar was lying on a stone in the garden. The sun was shining, and she was feeling warm and sleepy. She began to feel hungry, but she was too lazy to move to find her favourite food, which were leaves in the vegetable garden. The longer she stayed there the more hungry she became, but she was still too lazy to move. When she decided that she was so hungry that she would have to go and find some leaves to eat, she opened her eyes and discovered that it was night time and she could not find her way to the vegetable patch because it was too dark. Now she was very hungry and she was also cold because there was no sun to keep her warm.

Question

Do you think that it is wrong for Charlotte to be lazy?

If the children answer yes, ask them:
Why is it wrong for Charlotte to be lazy?

Possible reasons:

- You would never get anything done if you were always lazy.
- She did something that made her cold and hungry. Counterexample: you have been out playing in the snow and now you're cold and hungry. But have you done anything wrong?

OR

If the children answer no, ask them:
Why is it not wrong for Charlotte to be lazy?

Possible reasons:

- Sometimes it's nice to do nothing.
- When you're feeling sleepy, you're not lazy. Counterexample: if you felt sleepy all the time, and so never did anything, wouldn't you be lazy?

Story (continues)

The next day Charlotte decided to go down to the pond in the garden where she met Felicity the frog. 'Hello', said Charlotte. 'What are you doing?' 'I'm collecting flies to feed to my children. You could help me', said Felicity. 'Not me', said Charlotte. She was too lazy to help anyone. Felicity carried on collecting flies but she was not quick enough and her young frogs began to cry because they were so hungry. 'Please help me', called Felicity. But Charlotte refused. She just wanted to sit in the sunshine and was still too lazy to help. The young frogs had to wait, feeling very hungry and miserable, until Felicity had caught enough flies to feed them. It took her a very long time to do this.

Question

Do you now think that it is wrong for Charlotte to be lazy?

If the children answer yes, ask them:
Why is it wrong for Charlotte to be lazy?

Possible reasons:

- Others suffered because she didn't help.
- She was asked to help but didn't, and you should always help when you're asked. Counterexamples: (a) Someone asks you to help and you do so five times, is it wrong not to help them when they ask yet again? (b) Someone asks you to help them to do something wrong, e.g., to steal something.

OR

If the children answer no, ask them:
Why is it not wrong for Charlotte to be lazy?

Possible reasons:

- Being lazy is fun. Objection: doing something can be fun but still wrong.
- It was Felicity's job (responsibility) to feed her babies, not Charlotte's. Objection: Felicity's babies needed food and Charlotte could help.
- Charlotte was enjoying herself in the sun, so it is alright for her to be lazy. Counterexample: you are sitting in the sun and your friend has fallen over and hurt her knee. You don't do anything. Haven't you done something wrong?

Summary

First, state the question we have discussed: we have been talking about whether it is wrong to be lazy, either if it hurts (harms) only you or if it hurts (harms) others.

Second, summarise what the children have said. The possibilities include:

If your laziness hurts only yourself:

- It is wrong because you would never get anything done.
- It is not wrong because no one else is hurt.

If your laziness hurts other people:

- It is wrong because you are hurting someone else.
- It is not wrong because being lazy is fun.

Follow up activity

Divide the children into pairs. One child thinks of and acts out a scenario in which they are lazy. The second child then tries to reason with the first child not to be lazy. The children then swap roles.

Alternative version

You could substitute people for the animals. For instance, Charlotte has no food in the house and she is so lazy that she can't be bothered to go out shopping, so she ends up very hungry. The next day Felicity, her next door neighbour, asks Charlotte to help her with her shopping, since Felicity needs to buy food for her four young children. Charlotte refuses.

PANCAKE THE GREEDY RABBIT

Philosophical topic

Ethics – greed.

Aim

To get the children to discuss whether it is always wrong to be greedy.

Props

- Pancake the rabbit, Mark, Molly and Barbara (toys, pictures or cut out figures).
- Carrots and a lettuce.
- The story of Pancake the Greedy Rabbit, which is at the end of this enquiry.

Story

Read the story.

Question

Do you think that Pancake was greedy because he ate so much food?

If the children answer yes, ask them:

Why do you think that Pancake was greedy?

Possible reasons:

- He ate far more than he needed.
- He will get fat if he eats so much.
- He ate lots of food: two breakfasts and two dinners.

OR

If the children answer no, ask them:

Why do you think that Pancake was not greedy?

Possible reasons:

- He was hungry.
- He needed the food.
- He was freely given the food.

Question

Is it always wrong to be greedy?

If the children answer yes, ask them:
Why is it always wrong to be greedy?

Possible reasons:

- You are eating lots of food. Counterexample: if you were really, really hungry (starving) and you ate a lot of food would this make you greedy?
- It makes you ill. Counterexample: chickenpox makes you ill, but you haven't done anything wrong in catching it.
- It makes you fat. Counterexample: some children can eat lots and never get fat, isn't it wrong for them to be greedy?
- It leaves less food for others. Counterexample: if you went to a birthday party and you ate as much as five children, but there was still plenty of food left for the others, wouldn't you still be greedy?
- It shows you can't control yourself.

OR

If the children answer no, ask them:
Why is it not always wrong to be greedy?

Possible reasons:

- We have to eat. Objection: you can eat without being greedy.
- Eating a lot is a sign of good health. Objection: eating too much may make you sick.
- Eating a lot is fun.
- Being greedy doesn't harm anyone else. Counterexample: you eat so much food that there's none left for other people.

Follow up question: you've just said that it's not always wrong to be greedy; so can you tell me when it's not wrong to be greedy?

Possible answers:

- When no-one else is hurt (harmed), it's not wrong to be greedy.
- When you don't hurt (harm) yourself, it's not wrong to be greedy.
- When someone freely gives you lots of something, it's not wrong to accept it.
- When you have not eaten in a long time, it's not wrong to be greedy.

Summary

First, state the question we have discussed: we have been talking about whether it is always wrong to be greedy.

Second, summarise what the children have said. The possibilities include:
- Greed is always wrong because it makes you ill or it shows you can't control yourself.
- Greed is not always wrong: it's not wrong when the greedy person leaves plenty of food for others or doesn't become sick.

Follow up activity

Ask the children to sort the following scenarios into those in which someone is greedy and those in which someone isn't greedy, and to discuss their reasons. The scenarios can be presented as printed cards for the older children to sort themselves.
- Bill sat down at the table with his friends and ate all the cake himself.
- John has been working hard at digging all day, so eats two dinners at one go.
- Mary has been ill for a week and hasn't been able to eat, so she eats three dinners at one go.
- Julie asks her mum for more pocket money.
- Bob asks a child to put all her pocket money into the charity box.
- Susan does several jobs in the house in order to earn lots of money.

The story: Pancake the Greedy Rabbit

Pancake the rabbit loved to eat and eat, and he was always hungry. In his garden there were plenty of grass and dandelion leaves for him to munch on all day. Pancake's owner, Mark, also gave him a bowl of rabbit food every morning for breakfast and another bowl for dinner.

But Pancake wanted more to eat, so every morning he went into the garden next door where Molly gave him carrots for breakfast and every evening he went to visit Barbara who lived opposite who gave him a lettuce for his dinner.

This went on for a very long time until one day Mark was talking to Molly and discovered that she was giving Pancake carrots for breakfast, so he was having two breakfasts. Barbara then told Mark that she gave Pancake lettuce for dinner every day, so he was having two dinners.

Mark said that Pancake was only to have one breakfast and one dinner a day, so Molly and Barbara were to stop feeding him. Pancake felt very unhappy. He stayed in his own garden and munched away sadly.

Chapter 5

Aesthetics

Beauty, pictures and stories

BEAUTIFUL THINGS

Philosophical topic

Aesthetics – beauty.

Aim

To get the children to discuss what makes something beautiful.

Props

- Five pictures (of snow, pebbles, dirty hands, a chair and a broken chair) which are at the end of this enquiry. Or you can use your own pictures.
- A chart (heading for the first column: Picture; heading for the second column: All agree it is beautiful; heading for the third column: All agree it is not beautiful; heading for the fourth column: Some agree it is beautiful and some disagree.)

Question

Look at the pictures at the end of this enquiry. For each picture ask the children: do you think that this picture is of something beautiful? Record their answers on the chart.

Question

Show the children the pictures they all agreed are of something beautiful (second column). What makes these things beautiful?

Possible reasons:

- The colours are bright. (If you use a colour picture.)
- The patterns are nice.
- The chair looks good to sit on (it looks like it does its job well).
- I like looking at these things. Counterexample: you may like looking at things that are not beautiful, e.g., a monster (you could use the picture of the Cave Monster in this chapter).

Question

Show the children the pictures that they all agreed are of something that is not beautiful (third column). What makes these things not beautiful?

Possible reasons:

- The hands are dirty and disgusting.
- They look scary.
- The colours are dull.
- These are horrible patterns.
- The chair is damaged, so it doesn't look good to sit on (it looks like it doesn't do its job).
- I don't like looking at these things. Counterexample: you may not like looking at some things that are beautiful, e.g., some spiders and snakes.

Question

Show the children the pictures which some thought were of something beautiful and some thought were not (fourth column). Why do some of you think that these things are beautiful and some of you think that they are not beautiful?

Possible reasons:

- The chair looks comfortable to sit on and has a pretty pattern. Or the chair looks hard to sit on.
- The broken chair still looks nice. Or the broken chair doesn't look nice because you can't sit on it.
- The pebbles have a nice pattern and look smooth. Or the pebbles are dull and higgledy-piggledy.

Summary

First, state the question we have discussed: we have been talking about what makes something beautiful.

Second, summarise what the children have said. The possibilities include:

- Something may be beautiful because of its colours, or its shape, or because it looks like it does its job well (fulfils its function well).
- Something may be not beautiful because of its colours, or its shape or because it looks like it doesn't do its job well (doesn't fulfil its function well).
- Something is beautiful because we like looking at it.
- Something may be beautiful to some people and not to others, so we can't say what makes it beautiful.

Follow up activity

Ask the children to draw a picture of something they think is beautiful. Ask the other children whether they agree with them and to give reasons.

Snow

Pebbles

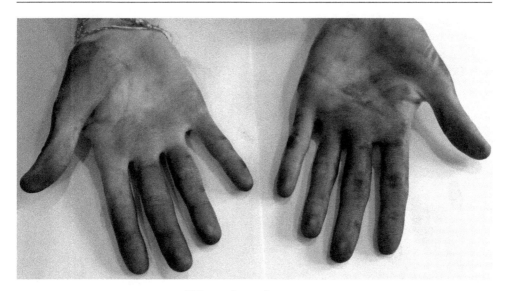

Dirty hands

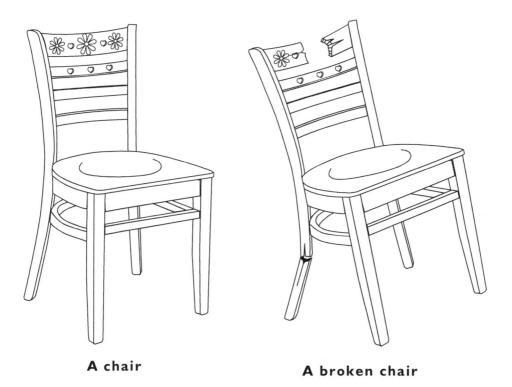

A chair   **A broken chair**

CATS

Philosophical topic

Aesthetics – photographs and drawings.

Aim

To get the children to discuss whether the subjects of a photograph and a drawing are real or imaginary.

Props

Four pictures, which are at the end of this enquiry.
- Picture 1: a photograph of a cat.
- Picture 2: a drawing of a cat cooking.
- Picture 3: a drawing of a real cat walking.
- Picture 4: a drawing of an imaginary cat sleeping.

Question

Show Picture 1. Say to the children: this is a photograph of a cat. Is it a picture of a real cat?

If the children answer yes, ask them:
How do you know that this cat is real?

Possible reasons:

- It looks like a real cat.
- It's a photograph, so there was a cat that was photographed.

OR

If the children answer no, ask them:
How do you know that this is not a real cat?

Possible reason:

- The cat isn't moving. Objection: the cat may have been moving, but the photograph only shows a moment in time.

Question

Show Picture 2. Say to the children: this is a drawing of a cat cooking. Is it a picture of a real cat?

If the children answer yes, ask them:
How do you know that this cat is real?

Possible reasons:

- It looks like a real cat. Objection: it's cooking and cats can't do that.
- The person drawing the cat must have looked at a real cat while drawing the picture. Objection: we can draw pictures of imaginary things, e.g., flying houses.

OR

If the children answer no, ask them:
How do you know that this cat is not real?

Possible reasons:

- This cat is cooking and cats can't do that.
- The cat isn't moving so it's not real. Objection: the cat may have been moving but when we make a drawing we only show a moment in time (remember what we said about the photograph).

Question

Show Pictures 3 and 4. Say to the children: these are two drawings. Picture 3 is a drawing of a real cat and Picture 4 is a drawing of an imaginary cat. I know this because the artist told me. If I hadn't told you, could you tell just by looking which of these cats is real and which is imaginary?

If the children answer yes, ask them:
How can you tell just by looking which cat is real and which cat is imaginary?

Possible reason:

- The cat in Picture 3 looks lively and is moving so it's real, and the cat in Picture 4 isn't lively or moving so it's imaginary. Objection: real cats sometimes don't look lively and go to sleep.

OR

If the children answer no, ask them:
Why can't you tell just by looking which cat is real and which cat is imaginary?

Possible reasons:

- We can draw things that are imaginary but they look like they are real, e.g., I can pretend to have a cat and then draw it.

- You need to be told by the artist whether the drawing is of a real or imaginary cat.

Summary

First, state the question we have discussed: we have been talking about whether photographs and drawings are of real or imaginary things.

Second, summarise what the children have said. The possibilities include:

- If it is a photograph, it is always of something real.
- If it is a drawing of something that couldn't really happen, then the drawing is of something imaginary.
- If it is a drawing of something that could happen, we can't tell just by looking whether it is of something real or imaginary. We need to ask the artist whether they were drawing something real or something imaginary (i.e., the artist's intentions matter in the case of drawings).

Follow up activity

Ask the children to draw or paint a picture of either a real or an imaginary thing. Tell them not to say which one they are going to do. Ask the other children if they can guess whether the pictures are of real or imaginary things.

Alternative version

Instead of cats, you can use as a subject another kind of thing that really exists, and you can use paintings instead of drawings, though you must also have one photograph.

A photograph of a cat

A drawing of a cat cooking

A drawing of a real cat walking

A drawing of an imaginary cat sleeping

A WALK ON THE BEACH

Philosophical topic
Aesthetics – fantasy and realistic stories.

Aim
To get the children to discuss the differences between fantasy and realistic fiction stories.

Props
- The two stories of A Walk on the Beach, which are at the end of this enquiry.

Story
Read Story 1.

Question
In this story Sam and Max walk on the beach. Max chases the gulls and Sam looks for fish. Is this a realistic story: a story about things which could have really happened? Or is it a fantasy story: a story about things which could never happen in real life?

If the children say that it is a realistic story, ask them:
Why do you think that the story is a realistic story?

Possible reasons:
- Dogs chase birds.
- The gulls would fly away when chased.
- We can look for fish in rock pools.
- We can take a dog for a walk on the beach.

OR

If the children say that it is a fantasy story, ask them:
Why do you think that the story is a fantasy story?

Possible reasons:

- This story is a made up one. Objection: realistic stories can be made up too. All fiction stories are made up, including realistic ones.
- Sam and Max don't exist. Objection: realistic stories can be about people who don't exist, but they are still about the kinds of things that can happen in real life. A boy walking on the beach with his dog is the kind of thing that can really happen.
- When we listen to this story, we imagine that the things in it happened, so this is a fantasy story. Objection: all fiction stories ask us to imagine (make-believe) things, including realistic fiction stories.

Story

Read Story 2.

Question

In this story Sam and Max walk on the beach. Max chases a dragon and talks to Sam. The sun also talks to Max. Is this a realistic story: a story about things which could have really happened? Or is it a fantasy story: a story about things which could never happen in real life?

If the children say that it is a realistic story, ask them:

Why do you think that the story is a realistic story?

Possible reason:

- We can walk on the beach with a dog in real life. Objections: (a) dogs can't talk and there are no dragons for them to chase; (b) some things that can happen in real life may happen in fantasy stories, but fantasy stories also contain some things that could never happen in real life.

OR

If the children say that it is a fantasy story, ask them:

Why do you think that the story is a fantasy story?

Possible reasons:

- Dragons do not exist.
- Animals do not talk.
- A dog could not jump that high.
- The sun cannot laugh or talk.

Summary

First, state the question we have discussed: we have been talking about how we can tell whether a (fictional) story is a realistic story or a fantasy story.

Second, summarise what the children have said. The possibilities include:

- In a realistic story the only things that happen are those that can happen in real life.
- In a fantasy story, anything at all can happen.
- In a fantasy story, some real things may happen as well as some things that can't happen in real life.
- There is no difference between realistic and fantasy stories since they are both made up.

Follow up activity

Ask the children either individually, in pairs or in small groups to write a realistic or a fantasy story. These can be read to the other children in the larger group, who then have to decide whether the story is realistic or fantasy, and give their reasons. Very young children will be able to make up stories with their teacher.

Story 1

It is a lovely sunny day and Sam is walking along the beach with Max his dog. 'Come on Max, let's see if we can find any fish in the rock pools', says Sam. They both run across the sand towards the rocks. But Max sees the gulls standing near the edge of the water. He runs towards them barking. The gulls are frightened and start to fly away. Max is trying to catch them, but they are too quick for him and soon Max is left standing on his own. 'Come back and stop chasing those birds', shouts Sam. 'You will never be able to catch them.' Max turns and runs to Sam, who is now looking in the pools. They search for fish, but do not find any. Sam looks up and sees that the sun is getting low in the sky. 'We had better go home because it will be dark soon', he tells Max. Sam runs back up the beach and Max runs beside him barking until they reach home.

Story 2

On another sunny day Sam and Max, his dog, are walking on the beach again. This time they are paddling in the sea. Sam looks up into the sky, stops, and looks harder. He says to Max, 'Look up there, what is that?' Max looks up. 'It's a dragon', replies Max, and starts to chase after it. The dragon looks down at the beach and shouts, 'You can't catch me.' Max is determined to catch the dragon. He runs really fast and suddenly when he is underneath the dragon he makes an enormous jump, which takes him right up into the clouds. He snaps at the dragon's tail but misses. The dragon flies on laughing. Max tries again with another enormous jump but the dragon is flying too fast for him to catch. 'Stop trying to catch the dragon', shouts Sam. 'No, I want to catch him and talk to him', shouts Max as he lands on the ground and runs faster down the beach. He tries a few more times to catch the dragon but does not succeed. Now the sun starts to laugh. 'You'll never catch that dragon, he flies too quickly for a little dog like you to catch', calls out the sun. Max is so surprised to hear the sun talking to him that he stops running, sits down and looks up at the sun. 'I didn't know you could talk', he says. 'Well you can talk, so why shouldn't I?' says the sun.

THE CAVE MONSTER

Philosophical topic

Aesthetics – enjoying scary stories.

Aim

To get the children to discuss how it's possible to enjoy scary stories, even though we don't enjoy fear in real life situations.

Props

- The illustrated story of The Cave Monster, which is at the end of this enquiry.
- A chart (heading for the first column: Name; heading for the second column: Enjoy being scared listening to scary stories; heading for the third column: Enjoy being scared in real life).

Story

Read the story.

Questions

Was that a scary story? Have you heard other scary stories? Do you enjoy being scared when you hear scary stories? For each child, write their name in the first column of the chart and record their answer to the last question in the second column.

Questions

Have you ever been scared in real life? Can you give some examples? Did you enjoy being scared in real life? For each child, record their answer to the last question in the third column of the chart.

Question

Referring to the chart, say to the children: some of you have said that you enjoy being scared when you listen to scary stories, but you don't enjoy being scared in real life. (If none of your children have said this, then replace 'some of you' with 'some people'.)

So what's the difference: why can you enjoy being scared when you're listening to scary stories, but not enjoy being scared in real life?

Possible reasons:

- In real life, when I'm scared I'm really in danger, but when I'm listening to a scary story I'm not really in danger. So I can enjoy being scared when listening to the story.
- When I'm listening to a story, I can decide to stop paying attention to the story, if it gets too scary. But in real life, I can't do anything about it, if something gets too scary.
- I wasn't really afraid when I was listening to the story, it was just pretend fear and I enjoy feeling that. But in real life I feel real fear and I don't enjoy feeling that.
- There's no difference: I don't enjoy being afraid in real life and I didn't enjoy being afraid when I listened to the story. I enjoyed something else about it, e.g., the monster was cool or I wanted to know what would happen.
- There's no difference: sometimes in real life I enjoy being scared, just like I enjoy being scared when I listen to a scary story, e.g., I enjoy scary rides at the fair.

Summary

First, state the question we have discussed: we have been talking about why we can enjoy being scared when listening to scary stories, even though we don't enjoy being scared in real life.

Second, summarise what the children have said. The possibilities include:

- In real life I'm in danger, but when I'm listening to stories I'm not.
- I can stop listening to a scary story, but in real life this won't help.
- I'm not really scared when listening to a scary story, it's just pretend fear.
- There's no difference: I don't enjoy being scared in real life and I don't enjoy being scared when listening to scary stories.
- There's no difference: sometimes I enjoy fear in real life, just like when listening to a scary story.

Follow up activity

Ask the children to write a scary story or draw a scary monster. Ask the other children whether they think the story or drawing is scary, and if so whether they enjoyed it and why.

The story: The Cave Monster

When Billy was walking along the beach he found the entrance to a cave. He took a step inside. It was cold and dark. Billy crept slowly forward, holding his hands out in front of him. He touched something wet and slimy, and screamed. But it was only a rock at the side of the cave.

He continued slowly towards the back of the cave. Suddenly he heard a shuffling sound and stopped to listen. The sound came closer and closer. An enormous dark shape moved towards him. In the dim light he saw two very large and sharp horns. Two big yellow eyes stared at him. Then two long, hairy arms began to stretch towards him. A deep voice boomed, 'What are *you* doing in my cave?'

Billy was so scared that he couldn't move. 'Are you a m.. m.. m.. monster?' he managed to ask. 'Of course I am! I catch anyone who comes into my cave and I put them in a large cage', roared the monster. The monster kept coming towards Billy, his long, blue tongue hanging out of his mouth.

Billy turned and ran wildly out of the cave to safety, as he heard the monster laughing and chanting, 'I frightened you! I frightened you!'

Chapter 6

Philosophy of mind

Emotions, beliefs and persons

PATCH AND HIS FRIENDS

Philosophical topic

Philosophy of mind – anger.

Aim

To get the children to discuss when it is right (appropriate) to be angry.

Props

- Patch, Rolly and Sandy (toys, pictures or cut outs).
- A chart (heading for the first column: Was Patch right to be angry?; heading for the second column: Was Patch wrong to be angry?; heading for the first row: Accident; heading for the second row: Teasing; heading for the third row: Hurting).
- Voting cards (e.g., a picture of a barking dog).

Story

Patch and his two friends, Rolly and Sandy, were playing with a ball in the garden. They were chasing after the ball when suddenly Patch tripped over a stone on the grass and hit his nose. It was very sore and he sat down and cried. When Rolly and Sandy ran back to see if he was hurt, Patch started to bark loudly at them, 'It's your fault that I fell over. My nose is sore. If you had not been running so fast, I wouldn't have fallen over.' He was very angry with his friends. Rolly and Sandy were shocked that they were getting the blame for something that was not their fault. It had been an accident that Patch had fallen over.

Question

Patch hurts himself and gets angry with Rolly and Sandy. Is Patch right to be angry? Get the children to vote and record their responses on the first row of the chart.

Story (continues)

Later when the dogs went into the house to have their tea, Sandy and Rolly began to tease Patch. Sandy barked, 'You were a cry baby when you hurt your nose.' 'We don't want to be your friend anymore, we don't like you', barked Rolly. Patch, whose nose was still hurting, began to get angry again. He didn't like being told that he was a cry baby and that the other two dogs did not like him. He rushed back out of the house into the garden.

Question

Rolly and Sandy tease Patch. Is Patch right to be angry? Get the children to vote and record their responses on the second row of the chart.

Story (continues)

Patch had calmed down and was lying in the sunshine when he heard a lot of barking and growling from the bottom of the garden. He ran to see what was happening. There beside the greenhouse Sandy was jumping on Rolly. Rolly was barking, 'Get off me, you're hurting me.' Sandy was paying no attention. He continued to jump on Rolly and was biting his ear. Patch stood still and barked his loudest bark, 'Stop that at once, can't you see that you're hurting Rolly?' He was very angry and continued to bark loudly until Sandy stopped.

Question

Rolly attacks Sandy just for fun. Is Patch right to be angry? Get the children to vote and record their responses on the third row of the chart.

Activity

Get the children to discuss the results recorded on the chart and to give their reasons for their answers. Point out, if it is the case, that some of them have said that Patch should be angry in some situations and not in others, and ask them to give their reasons for this difference.

Question

We have just discussed when it is right for Patch to be angry and when it is not right. Can you now tell me when is it right to be angry?

Possible answers:
- It is never right to be angry. Counterexample: what if getting angry is the only way to stop someone doing something horrible?
- It is right to be angry when someone has done something that you don't like. Counterexample: what if your mum tells you that you should go to bed because it's late? Should you be angry?
- It is right to be angry when it's the person's fault and not simply an accident.
- It is right to be angry when someone has done something wrong either to you or to someone else.

Summary

First, state the question we have discussed: we have been talking about when it is right (appropriate) to be angry.

Second, summarise what the children have said. The possibilities include:

- It is never right to be angry.
- It is right to be angry with someone when it's that person's fault and they have done something wrong, either to you or to someone else.

Follow up activity

Draw a picture of an angry person. Ask the children to tell the group why the person is angry or to write this under their picture. Get the group to discuss whether this is a good reason for the person to be angry.

RABBIT AND MOUSE

Philosophical topic

Philosophy of mind – fear.

Aim

To get the children to discuss when it is right (appropriate) to be afraid.

Props

- Rabbit and Mouse (toys, pictures or cut outs).

Story

Rabbit and Mouse were running happily between the trees in the wood when they heard a loud engine noise followed by an enormous crash. They stopped and looked at each other. 'I think that someone is cutting down trees', said Rabbit. 'I'm scared of that noise', said Mouse in a tiny voice. 'One of those trees might fall on us if we stay here', he added. 'I'm frightened too', whispered Rabbit. They turned and ran away very fast. Soon they were out of the woods and into the fields.

Question

Do you think that Mouse was right to be afraid?

If the children answer yes, ask them:

Why do you think that he was right to be afraid?

Possible reasons:

- Loud noises are frightening and this makes you move away.
- If the tree was about to fall on him that would be dangerous.
- Being frightened stopped him from being in danger.

OR

If the children answer no, ask them:

Why do you think that he was not right to be afraid?

Possible reasons:

- Nothing dangerous was going to happen to him.
- It was only a noise and noises can't hurt you.
- The noise was in the distance.

Story (continues)

Rabbit and Mouse were at the edge of a cabbage field. 'Oh good', said Rabbit. 'I'm really hungry. Let's stay here and eat some cabbages.' As they moved into the field Mouse gave a big scream and pointed to the middle of the field. 'Look, look', he stuttered, staring straight at a very large scarecrow standing among the cabbages. 'He looks very scary with those big eyes and long arms. I'm not going to stay here. He may run and catch me.' 'There's no need to be afraid. That scarecrow is just made of wood, clothes and vegetables', Rabbit told Mouse. 'I'm still scared', said Mouse. He ran away, leaving Rabbit to enjoy eating the cabbages on his own.

Question

Do you think that Mouse was right to be afraid?

If the children answer yes, ask them:
Why do you think that he was right to be afraid?

Possible reason:

- Mouse thought the scarecrow was alive and if he was, the scarecrow might have caught Mouse.

OR

If the children answer no, ask them:
Why do you think that he was not right to be afraid?

Possible reasons:

- It was only a scarecrow and he couldn't do anything to Mouse.
- When Mouse was told that the scarecrow was not alive, he was still afraid, even though he knew that the scarecrow couldn't hurt him.
- By running away, Mouse could not get anything to eat and he needs food.

Question

Most of the children will say that Mouse was right to be afraid when he heard the noise and not right to be afraid when he saw the scarecrow. If they say this, ask them:

Why was it right for Mouse to be afraid when he heard the noise but not when he saw the scarecrow?

Possible reason:

- Mouse might have been hurt by falling trees, but he couldn't be hurt by a scarecrow.

Question

Now can you now tell me when it is right to be afraid?

Possible answers:

- It is never right to be afraid. Objection: if we never felt fear, we would not avoid dangerous situations, so we would get hurt a lot.
- It is right to be afraid when the situation only seems dangerous. Objection: if it only seems dangerous and we run away, we might not be able to get something good.
- It is right to be afraid when the situation really is dangerous, but not right when it only seems dangerous.

Summary

First, state the question we have discussed: we have been talking about when is it right (appropriate) to feel afraid.

Second, summarise what the children have said. The possibilities include:

- It is right to feel afraid when the situation really is dangerous, but not right when it only seems dangerous.
- It is never right to feel afraid.

Follow up activity

Divide the children into groups, and ask each group to think of several situations when they might feel afraid. Then ask them to discuss whether it is right to be afraid in these situations or not.

HAPPY SUZY

Philosophical topic

Philosophy of mind – happiness.

Aim

To get the children to discuss what makes us happy.

Props

- The story of Happy Suzy, which is at the end of this enquiry.
- A chart (heading for the first column: Name; heading for the second column: What makes me happy; heading for the third column: Number).
- Two sets of voting cards, one of happy faces and one of sad faces.

Story

Read the story.

Question

What things make Suzy happy?

Answers:

- Getting invited to a birthday party.
- Buying and giving presents.
- Dressing up in her party dress.
- Eating delicious food.
- Going to sleep when she's tired.

Activity

Ask each child for something which makes them happy. Record the child's name in the first column and their answer in the second column of the chart. Read out each answer and ask the children to vote with their happy or sad cards about whether this would make them happy or not. Record the number of children who say that it would make them happy in the third column. Point out, if this is the case, that there are some things that make all of us happy and some things that make only some of us happy.

Question

Why do the things on our chart make us happy?

Possible reasons:

- We are doing things that we like to do.
- We are with our friends or family.
- We are helping others.
- We are giving presents to others.
- We are getting presents from others.
- We are eating our favourite food.
- We are playing with toys.

Question

Do you think that all of the things that make us happy have something in common?

If the children answer yes, ask them:
Why do you think that they all have something in common?

Possible reasons:

- All of them are things that give us pleasure.
- All of them are things that we want.
- All of them are things that we need.

OR

If the children answer no, ask them:
Why do you think that they do not have something in common?

Possible reasons:

- They are very different: for example, some are things, some are activities and some are people. Some are things we need and some are things we want.
- Different things make different people happy.

Summary

First, state the question we have discussed: we have been talking about what makes us happy.
Second, summarise what the children have decided. The possibilities include:

- Things make us happy because we want or need or enjoy them.
- Each of us is made happy by many different things and they have nothing in common.
- Different people are made happy by different things.

Follow up activity

Ask the children in pairs to make a list of six things that make them happy and one thing that does not make them happy. Read these lists out to the other children and ask them to find the odd one out, the one that does not make them happy. Ask them to explain why they think that this is the odd one out.

The story: Happy Suzy

Suzy comes running into the kitchen when she gets home from school. 'Look Mum, I've got an invitation to Mary's birthday party. Please say I can go', she says. 'Of course you can go', her mum replies. Suzy is jumping up and down, she is so happy.

'Now we need to buy Mary a lovely present. It makes me really happy buying and giving presents. When can we go?' asks Suzy. Her mum laughs. 'You will have to wait until Saturday', her mum tells her.

When the day of the party arrives Suzy puts on her party dress. 'This dress always makes me feel happy', she tells her mum.

Mary's mum has provided a birthday tea with lots of things that Suzy likes to eat. 'Oh look at all this food. I'm feeling really hungry', says Suzy. Sitting down at the table she thanks Mary's mum and says, 'I'm so happy eating all this delicious food.'

Suzy really enjoys the party. When she gets home she is very tired and is happy to go to bed when it is bedtime.

SAD TEDDY

Philosophical topic

Philosophy of mind – sadness.

Aim

To get the children to discuss what makes us sad.

Props

- Teddy with a hankie.
- Voting cards with sad faces.

Question

Teddy is feeling very sad. He is crying and using his hankie to dry his tears. Why do you think that he's sad? List the children's answers on the board.

Possible reasons:

- He's fallen over and hurt himself.
- His mum has left him.
- His friends are being nasty to him.
- Someone has taken his toy away.
- He's been made to eat something he doesn't want to eat.
- He has got very cold.
- He's been told he can't go out to play.
- He's feeling bad because he's done something wrong.

Question

Do the things that make teddy sad also make you sad?

Read through the answers, asking the children to hold up their voting cards if the thing listed also makes them sad. Record the number of children who feel sad against each answer.

Question

See if you can encourage the children to generalise their answers. Ask them in what ways can we group together the different things that make us sad? Write down the children's answers on the board.

Possible groups:
- Things to do with our bodies (sensations), e.g., having toothache, being cold, being in pain, or feeling hungry.
- Feelings (emotions), e.g., feeling guilt, anger or fear.
- Friends and family, e.g., having no friends to play with or your mum has left you.
- Things that we own, e.g., someone has taken away our toys or the toy is broken.
- Having to do things, e.g., having to go to bed when we don't want to.
- Not being able to do things, e.g., not being able to go outside to play.

Activity

Say to the children: let's see if we can group the answers to the last question about what makes us sad under these two headings (write them on the board):
- When we have something that we don't want (e.g., toothache or when a friend is being unkind).
- When we don't have something that we do want (e.g., we don't have food when we are hungry or we can't go out to play).

Summary

First, state the question we have discussed: we have been talking about what makes us sad.
Second, summarise what the children have done:
- We have listed the particular things that make us sad, e.g., having to go to bed early, getting very cold, etc.
- We have grouped together the things that make us sad, e.g., as things to do with our bodies, friends and family, etc.
- We have seen that the things that make us sad are either things that we have but don't want, or things that we don't have but want.

Follow up activity

Ask the children to draw a picture of a sad person. Each child can tell the group why the person is sad and then the child can ask for suggestions about how to make the person in the picture happy.

ANDY'S ACCIDENT

Philosophical topic

Philosophy of mind – pain.

Aim

To get the children to discuss whether feeling pain is always a bad thing.

Props

- Andy (a doll or a cut out figure).
- A bandage.
- A wall, which could be made from a box.

Story

Andy is mending a wall. He is sitting on top of the wall putting the last few bricks in place when he hears his friend shout from below, 'Hello Andy.' Andy turns quickly, loses his footing, stumbles and falls. He lands in a heap on the ground. His friend rushes over, 'Have you hurt yourself?' he asks anxiously. Andy groans, 'My knee is very sore, look it's beginning to swell up.' His friend looks at the knee and goes to the first–aid box to find a bandage. 'I'll put on this bandage and then I'll take you to the doctor.'

Question

Andy is in a lot of pain, how is he feeling?

Possible answers:

- Very sore.
- Frightened.
- Tearful.
- Unhappy.

Question

Is pain always a bad thing?

If the children answer yes, ask them:
Why is pain always bad?

Possible reasons:

- We don't like to feel pain.
- Pain makes us cry.
- When we feel pain it puts us in a bad mood.

Counterexample: you've said that pain is always a bad thing, but if we did not feel pain, we would not learn to avoid things that are dangerous, such as touching a hot cooker.

OR

If the children answer no, ask them:
Why is pain not always bad?

Possible reasons:

- We learn to be careful so that we don't fall or injure ourselves.
- We learn not to touch dangerous things, like hot cookers.
- Once we have injured ourselves we know to stop moving, which will stop the injury getting worse.
- Sometimes mum gives us something nice and comforts us when we feel pain.

Question

Pain is bad, because we don't like it, and pain is also good, because it stops us from injuring ourselves. But how can something be both bad and good at the same time?

Possible answer:

- Pain is bad in itself, since we don't like it. But pain also has good effects: it stops us from injuring ourselves. (We've made a distinction.)

Summary

First, state the question we have discussed: we have been talking about whether pain is always a bad thing.
Second, summarise what the children have said. The possibilities include:

- Pain is bad because we don't like the feeling of pain.
- Pain is good because it teaches us not to hurt ourselves.
- Pain is bad in itself but it has good effects.

Follow up activities

- Divide the children into groups and ask them to think of three situations where they might feel pain. Discuss whether the pain in each case was a good or bad thing.

- Ask the children whether they can think of some other things, besides pain, that are bad in themselves but have good effects. (Examples: your mum tells you off to stop you running into the road again; or you get scared climbing a dangerous tree and decide to go back down.)

GIANTS

Philosophical topic

Philosophy of mind – pretending and believing.

Aim

To get the children to discuss whether pretending to be something requires them to believe that they are that thing.

Activity

Discuss with the children what giants are: how they move and how they speak. Then ask the children to move around, pretending to be giants.

Question

Once the children are sitting back in the circle say this to them. You were all pretending to be giants. I'm going to ask you whether you also *believed* you were giants. When we believe something, we think it's true. So did you really *believe* you were giants?

If the children answer yes, ask them:

Why do you think you believed you were giants?

Possible reasons:

- It was fun to believe it. Objection: if you believe something, you think it's true. But just because something would be fun to believe doesn't make it true. So did you really believe you were a giant?
- When I'm pretending to be something, I have to think very hard, so I believe I'm that thing. Objection: can't you just imagine you're that thing, without believing you are?
- Giants have big arms and legs, walk in big steps and speak in deep voices; and I have big arms and legs, walk in big steps and speak in a deep voice.

Counterexample: you've said that you believed you were giants; now pretend to be a star in the sky. Do you really believe you are a star in the sky? If so, why are you still here in the room?

OR

If the children answer no, ask them:

Why do you think you did not believe you were giants?

Possible reasons:

- When I looked down at my feet and legs, they were just normal size.
- When I look in a mirror, I can see I'm not a giant.
- If we were all giants, how would we fit into the room?
- Giants don't really exist, so I didn't believe I was one. Follow up question: if I asked you to pretend you were something that really exists, like a butterfly, would you believe you were one?

Summary

First, state the question we have discussed: we have been talking about whether when you pretend to be something, you also believe you are that thing.

Second, summarise what the children have said. The possibilities include:

- When we pretend to be something, we believe we are that thing, since it's fun to believe it, or we're thinking hard about what we're pretending to be (we're absorbed in it).
- When we pretend to be something, we don't believe we are that thing, since we can see we're not that thing, or we can't do the things we're pretending to do, or the thing doesn't exist.

Follow up activity

Get the children to pretend they are something that really exists, e.g., an elephant. Ask them whether they really believed that they were elephants.

ISAAC THE ROBOT

Philosophical topic

Philosophy of mind – persons.

Aim

To get the children to discuss whether a robot without feelings or thoughts could be a person.

Props

- The illustrated story of Isaac the Robot, which is at the end of this enquiry.

Story

Read the story.

Question

Is Isaac the Robot a person?

If the children answer yes, ask them:
Why do you think that Isaac the Robot is a person?

Possible reasons:
- He talks just like us and can answer questions correctly. Counterexample: a computer can answer some questions correctly, but is it a person?
- He does things like us.
- He moves around and dances. Counterexample: butterflies move around but they are not persons.
- He can make things. Counterexample: spiders make webs, and machines in factories make things, but they are not persons.

OR

If the children answer no, ask them:
Why do you think that Isaac the Robot isn't a person?

Possible reasons:

- He's made of metal but a person is made of skin and bones. Counterexample: couldn't there be an alien from another planet who is a person but not made from skin and bones?
- He's only a machine.
- He doesn't feel pain, but a person does. Counterexample: some people can't feel pain (a rare genetic disorder).
- He doesn't feel happy or sad, but we do. Counterexample: sometimes when you're asleep you don't feel anything, but you're still a person.
- He doesn't have any thoughts, but we do.
- He doesn't eat. Objection: food gives us energy and batteries give Isaac energy.

Summary
First, state the question we have discussed: we have been talking about whether a robot without feelings or thoughts could be a person.
Second, summarise what the children have said. The possibilities include:

- Isaac the Robot is a person, since he acts like you and me, he can answer questions correctly and can make things.
- Isaac the Robot isn't a person, since he doesn't feel anything and has no thoughts.

Follow up activity
Ask the children to draw one alien from another planet who is a person, and another alien who isn't a person. Ask them to explain the differences.

The story: Isaac the Robot

This is a picture of Isaac, who is a robot. He is made of metal and runs on batteries. When you talk to Isaac, he'll answer you. If you ask him his name, he'll say, 'Isaac'. If you want to know something, he'll tell you the answer. If he falls over and damages his knee, he'll hold it and cry, 'Oh, oh, my knee!' When he hears music, he starts to dance. If you need a chair or a teddy, he'll make one for you. He's a very clever robot.

When I spoke to the man who made Isaac, he told me that Isaac doesn't have any thoughts in his head. And when he falls over and says, 'Oh, oh, my knee!' he doesn't feel any pain. When he's dancing, he doesn't feel happy or sad or anything at all. He does things like you and me, but he doesn't think or feel anything.

Chapter 7

Epistemology
Dreams and illusions

MILLY'S BAD DREAM

Philosophical topic

Epistemology – dreams and reality.

Aim

To get the children to discuss how they know that the things in their dreams do not really happen at the time they are dreaming.

Props

- The story of Milly's Bad Dream, which is at the end of this enquiry.
- Milly (a doll or a cut out).
- A box to use as a bed.

Story

Read the story.

Question

Milly thinks that everything in her dream really happened. How did her mum persuade her that the things in her dream did not really happen?

Answers:

- Mum said that pink fluffy creatures do not exist.
- Mum showed her that her room was tidy.
- Mum said that she had not heard any shouting.

Activity

Like Milly do you dream? Tell the group about a dream you have had.

Question

When you wake up how do you know that the things in your dream did not really happen?

Possible answers:

- If you can find them, ask the people who appeared in your dream whether what you dreamt about really happened.

- Ask your mum and dad, if they have been in the house all the time with you, whether the things in your dream really happened.
- See if anything has been changed in a way that happened in your dream.
- Ask yourself if there were things in your dream that don't exist.
- Ask yourself whether things really could happen in the ways they happened in your dream.

Summary

First, state the question we have discussed: we have been talking about how we know that the things in our dreams did not really happen.

Second, summarise what the children have said. The possibilities include:

- We can ask anyone who appeared in our dream whether these things really happened.
- We can ask anyone who was with us when we were asleep whether what we dreamt about really happened.
- We can look for evidence for whether things really changed in ways that they did in our dream.
- We can ask whether things that were in our dream really exist.
- We can think about whether things that happened in our dream really could happen.

Follow up activity

Ask the children to draw a picture of something which could only happen to them in a dream. Ask the children to show these pictures to the others and discuss why this could only happen in a dream.

The story: Milly's Bad Dream

Milly was sound asleep in her bed. She heard a strange noise. She sat up and saw her bedroom door opening and in came two little pink fluffy creatures. They climbed onto her bed and shouted, 'Hello Milly.' Milly didn't say anything, she was feeling frightened.

The creatures jumped off her bed and ran around the room shouting. They opened her drawers and took out all her clothes, throwing them onto the floor, laughing.

'Stop that!' Milly shouted, but they paid no attention to her. The creatures continued to make a mess of her bedroom by scattering all her toys. Then with a big shout they scuttled out of the door.

'Mum, Mum!' Milly cried. Her mum came running into the bedroom. 'What's wrong?' she asked. 'Oh Mum there were two pink fluffy creatures in my room and they were making a terrible mess and shouting very loudly', Milly told her.

'I think you were dreaming. There are no pink fluffy creatures at all and certainly they have not been here. Look around the room, Milly, can you see a mess?' asked her mum. 'No, there's no mess', replied Milly.

'Did you not hear them shouting?' Milly asked. Mum replied, 'No, and I would have heard them because I was quietly reading my book.'

'I must have been dreaming and none of these things really happened', agreed Milly.

DREAMING OF SCHOOL

Philosophical topic

Epistemology – are you dreaming now?

Aim

To get the children to discuss how they know that they are not dreaming now.

Props

- The story, Dreaming of School, which is at the end of this enquiry.

Story

Read the story.

Question

Tom thought he was at school, but then realised it was only a dream. Next day he seems to be at school, but he is suddenly puzzled about whether he is only dreaming this or whether he really is at school. How do you know that you are really here at school and not at home in bed, dreaming that you are here in school?

Possible reasons:

- We can see that we are here in this room. Counterexample: sometimes we dream that we see something, e.g., Tom dreamt that he looked at his books.
- We can touch and feel things in this room. Counterexample: sometimes we dream that we are touching something.
- We can discuss with the other children and agree that we are all in this room. Counterexample: we may only be dreaming that we are talking with the other children, just as Tom dreamt that he talked with his friends.
- We remember that we woke up this morning and got out of bed. Counterexample: sometimes we dream that we have woken up but we are still asleep.
- We don't know that we are not dreaming: everything we seem to see and touch may only be in our dream. Follow up question: how can we know anything about the world, since everything we experience might be a dream?

Summary

First, state the question we have discussed: we have been talking about how we know that we are not dreaming now.

Second, summarise what the children have said. The possibilities include:

- We know that we are not dreaming now because we can see and feel things around us, we remember waking up this morning and we can ask other children.
- We do not know that we are not dreaming now because everything we think we see and feel around us may only be something that we are dreaming.

Follow up activity

Ask the children to tell the others about their most lifelike (realistic) dreams. Then get them to discuss the ways in which the dreams are like real life and the ways in which they are different.

The story: Dreaming of School

Tom was dreaming that he was in school. He looked at his books, listened to the teacher, drew pictures and talked to his friends. Later he woke up in his bed and was very surprised. 'I thought I was in school', he said. 'I didn't realise I was dreaming. It was just as if I was there.'

Next day Tom went to school, he looked at his books, listened to the teacher, drew pictures and talked to his friends. Suddenly he was puzzled. He thought, 'It's just like in my dream. How do I know that I'm not still in my bed and dreaming all of this?'

A STICK IN THE WATER

Philosophical topic

Epistemology – visual illusions.

Aim

To get the children to discuss how we know that some things we see are visual illusions.

Props

- A clear container filled with water.
- A pencil or any rigid stick.

Story

Bill and Sam are very excited because their teacher has promised to show them an experiment. 'I wonder what she will show us', says Sam. 'Here she comes. Look she has a big bowl of water, perhaps we will get wet', answers Bill. 'Hello', their teacher greets them. 'Wait until you see what I have to show you. I think that you will be fascinated.' The teacher holds a pencil partly in the bowl of water and shows the boys that the part of the pencil that is in the water appears to be bent. (Demonstrate this to your children.) 'Look, the pencil in the water is bent', cries Bill. 'Don't be silly, of course the pencil is not bent, it only looks bent', replies Sam. But Bill insists, 'It is bent. If you can see that it's bent, then of course it's bent!'

Question

Do you think that Bill is right, that if you see something as being a certain way, then it really is that way?

If the children answer yes, ask them:
Why do you think Bill is right?

Possible reason:
- When we see something as being a certain way, it really is that way, for instance, we see that there's a pencil in front of us and there is one there.

Objection: things usually look the way they are, but not always, e.g., it looks as if the earth ends at the horizon, but it carries on beyond it.

OR

If the children answer no, ask them:
Why do you think Bill was not right?

Possible reason:

- Sometimes our senses (seeing, feeling, etc) mislead us, e.g., when someone walks away from you, they seem to get smaller, but they don't really get smaller.

Story (continues)

Sam replies, 'No the pencil isn't bent. What you are seeing is a visual illusion. Do you know what a visual illusion is?' Bill shakes his head. Sam continues, 'A visual illusion is when something looks a certain way but it isn't really like that. The pencil looks like it's bent in the water, but it's still straight. And I can prove this to you: when I lift it out of the water you can see that it's straight.' (Demonstrate this to your children.) Bill says, 'I disagree. I can see that the pencil is straight when it's out of the water but I can also see that the pencil is bent when it's in the water. So it must bend when we put it in the water. This isn't an illusion.' Sam replies, 'Pencils don't bend. And if you run your hand down the pencil when it's in the water, you'll feel that it's straight. You try it Bill.' (Get your children to do this.)

Question

Do you think that Bill is right, does the pencil bend when it is put in the water and straighten when it comes out of the water?

If the children answer yes, ask them:
Why do you think that Bill is right?

Possible reasons:

- Maybe this is a trick pencil that does bend. Objection: we can find out that it's not a trick pencil by trying to bend it.
- Maybe it's touch that's misleading us and not sight. Touch can mislead us, e.g., putting your hands in bowls of water at different temperatures (see follow up activity).

OR

If the children answer no, ask them:
Why do you think that Bill is not right?

Possible reasons:

- We can try to bend the pencil and find out that it won't bend.

- When we take the pencil out of the water, we can see that it's straight.
- Running our hand down the pencil shows us that it's still straight when it's in the water. Sometimes we use touch to tell us how things are when seeing misleads us, e.g., we think the cooker is cool when we look at it, but discover by touch that it's still hot!

Summary

First, state the question we have discussed: we have been talking about how we know that some things we see are visual illusions.

Second, summarise what the children have said. The possibilities include:

- There are no visual illusions.
- We know that something is a visual illusion because we can use other senses such as touch to tell us what the thing is really like.
- We know that something is a visual illusion because we know facts about things, e.g., we know that the pencil is normal so it won't bend in water.
- We know that something is a visual illusion because we can vary the conditions under which we observe things, e.g., taking the pencil out of the water.

Follow up activities

- Get the children to experiment with different items to see if they appear to bend in the water.
- Find other examples of visual illusions to show the children, e.g., the Müller-Lyer illusion. There are many examples on the internet.
- Try this experiment: put your right hand in a bowl of hot water and your left hand in a bowl of cold water for a minute. Then put both hands in a bowl of lukewarm water: it will feel cool to your right hand and warm to your left hand.

Chapter 8

Metaphysics

What is real?

ANGUS THE CAT

Philosophical topic

Metaphysics – do the animals in a story really exist?

Aim

To get the children to think about the difference between real things and things that are not real by discussing how they know whether the animals in a story are real or not real.

Props

- The illustrated story of Angus the Cat, which is at the end of this enquiry.
- The drawing of a real cat, which is also at the end of this enquiry.

Story

Read the story.

Question

Do you think that the animals in the story are real animals?

If the children answer yes, ask them:
Why do you think that the animals are real?

Possible reasons:

- Angus looks like a cat, and Jake and Jack look like rabbits. Counterexample: a puppet of a cat looks like a cat but isn't a real cat, and puppets of rabbits look like rabbits but are not real rabbits.
- The animals get hungry and want something to eat like real animals do.
- The animals are running and walking in the story like real animals do. Objection (also to the reason above): they are also doing things like talking and playing football that real animals can't do.

OR

If the children answer no, ask them:
Why do you think that the animals are not real?

Possible reasons:
- These animals are in a story, so they cannot be real. Counterexample: real animals can be in a story, e.g., we could write a story about your hamster.
- These animals have been drawn. Counterexample: you can draw real animals (show the children the drawing of the real cat).
- The animals are not real because they are doing things that real animals can't do.

Follow up question: what are the animals doing that real animals can't do?
- They are wearing clothes. Counterexample: you can dress your own rabbit in clothes.
- They are eating cookies. Counterexample: we give real dogs cookies.
- They live in houses. Counterexample: real dogs and cats live in our houses.
- They are playing football: real animals can play with balls but they can't play football, since they can't understand the rules.
- They are speaking words and understand each other, but real animals can't, e.g., a parrot speaks but doesn't understand the meaning of the words.
- Angus's mum is baking.

Summary

First, state the question we have discussed: we have been talking about how we know whether the animals in a story are real or not real.

Second, summarise what the children have said. The possibilities include:
- The animals in the story are not real because they are doing some things that real animals can't do.
- The animals in the story are not real because they are drawings.
- The animals in the story are real because they are doing some things that real animals can do.

Follow up activity

Ask the children to draw their own pictures of animals that are not real. When they show these pictures to the group, ask the other children to say why the animals are not real.

The story: Angus the Cat

Angus the cat is running down the lane looking for his friends, Jake and Jack the rabbits. When he sees Jake and Jack coming out of their house he shouts, 'Shall we play football?' 'Yes', they both reply.

They continue down the lane until they come to the football field. They play football together until Jake says, 'I'm tired and need something to eat.' Angus agrees and says, 'Let's go to my house.'

When they get back to his house, Angus's mum has just made delicious chocolate cookies. 'Would you like one of these cookies?' his mum asks. 'Yes please', they yell. 'Be very careful, they are still hot from the oven', she warns. Angus, Jake and Jack stand around the table eating cookies until they are full.

Drawing of a real cat

NUMBERS

Philosophical topic

Metaphysics – are numbers real?

Aim

To get the children to discuss whether numbers are real.

Props

- The story, Numbers, which is at the end of this enquiry.
- Pencils.

Story

Read the story.

Question

John says that numbers are not real and Penny says that they are real. Do you think that numbers are real?

If the children answer yes, ask them:

Why do you think that numbers are real?

Possible reasons:

- Some things that are real can't be seen or touched, e.g., sounds and your thoughts.
- Some things that are real aren't at any place, e.g., the school rules. The written rules are somewhere, but you could tear them up and the rules would still exist. So the written rules are not the same as the rules.
- Numbers are real because we can use them to count up things in the real world and doing this gives us the right answers.
- We can write down numbers and then we can see and touch them, and also point to them, so they are real. Objection: these are written numbers (numerals), but they are not the same as numbers. We can erase the written numbers and they would be gone. But even if we did that, we could still count.

OR

If the children answer no, ask them:
Why do you think that numbers are not real?

Possible reasons:
- Everything that is real can be seen or touched. Counterexamples: (a) what about sounds, can you see or touch them? (b) your thoughts are real, but can you see or touch them?
- Everything that is real is somewhere and we can point to it, e.g., the pencil is there in front of us. But the numbers aren't anywhere – you can't point to where they are. Counterexample: not everything that is real is at some place, e.g., where are the school rules?
- Numbers are not real, since they are just thoughts in our heads. Objections: (a) if you stop thinking about numbers, does that mean that they no longer exist? (b) aren't thoughts in our heads real?
- Numbers are only imaginary, but they still tell us about the real world, since some things that we imagine tell us about the real world. For example, we can understand how other people are feeling by imagining how we would feel if we were them.

Summary

First, state the question we have discussed: we have been talking about whether numbers are real.
Second, summarise what the children have said. The possibilities include:
- Numbers are real, because we can see and touch them, and point to them, when we write them down.
- Numbers are real because they tell us true things about the real world; but they are different from things like pencils, because we can't see or touch them, and they aren't at any place. (They are abstract objects.)
- Numbers are not real, they are only imaginary, since we can't see or touch them, or point to them.

Follow up activity

Ask the youngest children to draw five teddies and write the number 5 next to them. (You can choose any number and item.) Ask the older children to make a number book for younger children, e.g., a book with a picture of one teddy with the numeral 1 next to it, two teddies with 2 next to it, and so on.

Alternative version

You can count things other than pencils! Use different numbers depending on the age of the children: try $2+1=3$ for the youngest children.

The story: Numbers

Penny and John enjoy counting. 'Let's count some pencils', said Penny. 'Good idea', said John. 'There are three pencils on this table', he said. 'And there are seven pencils on that table', said Penny. Then John thought a bit and looked puzzled. 'I can see and touch the pencils', he said. 'But I can't see and touch the numbers three and seven. When something is real, I can see and touch it. So numbers can't be real. Also when something is real, we can say where it is. But you can't show me where the numbers are. So numbers can't be real. They are only imaginary, like the imaginary, talking animals in storybooks.'

'That can't be right', replied Penny. 'Numbers are real because they tell us true things about the real world. If we put together our pencils, we know that we will have ten pencils, because 3+7=10. I don't have to count the pencils again to know that. So numbers tell us true things about the real world. But if a cow talks in a story, it doesn't tell us that real cows talk. So numbers are real, but they are different from things like pencils, since you can't touch or feel them, or point to them. They're different, but they are just as real.'

THESEUS'S SHIP

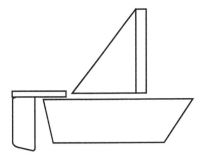

Philosophical topic

Metaphysics – when are things the same?

Aim

To get the children to discuss whether something is still the same object, even if each part has been replaced.

Props

- Two identical ships, each made of a hull, a rudder and a sail. Make the ships from cardboard cut outs (see the end of this enquiry for a template). Use one of the ships as Theseus's ship in the harbour. Use the other one, separated into its three parts, as the replacement parts in the boatshed.
- One sheet of blue paper (for the harbour) and one sheet of brown paper (for the boatshed).

Story

Theseus looks at his ship in the harbour. 'I think that the rudder is getting a bit old. I'll get one from my boatshed to replace it', he says. Theseus takes the old rudder off his ship and walks over to the boatshed where he leaves this rudder. He brings the replacement rudder back to his ship and fixes it on. (Do this with the cut outs.)

Question

The ship has a new rudder, so is the ship still Theseus's original ship? (The children are likely to answer yes.)

If the children answer yes, ask them:

Why is this Theseus's original ship?

Possible reason:

- Changing a part of something doesn't make it a different thing, e.g., changing your front door doesn't mean that you have a different house. Even replacing more than one part still doesn't make it a different thing, e.g., if we replace all the windows as well as the door, you still have the same house.

OR

If the children answer no, ask them:
Why is this not Theseus's original ship?

Possible reason:

- It has a new part, which is different from the part on the original ship. Counterexample: if mum and dad replace a tyre on the car, isn't it still the same car? Even if they replace more than one part, e.g., all of the tyres and also the engine, isn't it still the same car?

Story (continues)

Theseus stands back and looks at his ship. 'That's a smart rudder but I think that I need a new sail now', he says. So he takes down his sail and goes back to his boatshed where he leaves the sail and returns with the replacement sail to put on his ship. (Do this with the cut outs.)

Question

The ship now has a new rudder and a new sail, so is the ship still Theseus's original ship? (The children are likely to answer yes.)

Use again the 'if the children answer yes/no' dialogue and possible reasons above.

Story (continues)

This time when Theseus looks at his ship he says, 'That new rudder and sail make the hull of my ship look very scruffy, so I think I'll replace it with the hull I have in my boatshed.' He hauls the ship out of the harbour, takes off the hull, which he places in his boatshed, and puts on the replacement hull. Theseus then drags the ship back into the harbour. He is very pleased at how well the ship looks. (Do this with the cut outs.)

Question

The ship now has a new rudder, a new sail and a new hull. Is this still Theseus's original ship? (The children are likely to answer yes.)

Use again the 'if the children answer yes/no' dialogue and possible reasons above.

Story (continues)

Theseus goes back into his boatshed and looks at the rudder, sail and hull that he has put there. 'I could make a ship from these', he says. He takes the hull, puts up the sail and puts on the rudder to make a ship. (Do this with the cut outs.)

Question

Is the ship in the boatshed Theseus's original ship or is the one in the harbour his original ship?

If the children say that the ship in the boatshed is Theseus's original ship, ask them:

Why is the ship in the boatshed Theseus's original ship?

Possible reasons:

- It's made of exactly the same parts as Theseus's original ship that was in the harbour.
- All he has really done is move his original ship gradually to the boatshed.

Objection: replacing a part doesn't make the ship a new ship, and at each stage we've only replaced one part until we've replaced them all, so the ship in the harbour is Theseus's original ship. (If the children agreed at each stage that the ship in the harbour was Theseus's original ship, you should also remind them of this.) And the ship in the harbour is different from the one in the boatshed. So the ship in the boatshed can't be Theseus's original ship.

OR

If the children say that the ship in the harbour is Theseus's original ship, ask them:

Why is the ship in the harbour Theseus's original ship?

Possible reasons:

- We agreed at each stage of replacing the parts that the ship in the harbour was Theseus's original ship.
- Replacing its parts doesn't mean that the whole thing becomes a different thing, e.g., replacing tyres on a car, or replacing windows in a house, or giving teddy new eyes doesn't mean that there is now a different car, house or teddy.

Objection: the ship in the boatshed has been made with all the parts that Theseus took from his original ship, so it must be his original ship, not the one in the harbour.

OR

If the children say that the ship in the boatshed and the ship in the harbour are both Theseus's original ship, ask them:

Why are both the ship in the boatshed and the ship in the harbour Theseus's original ship?

Possible reason:

- The ship in the boatshed is made of the original parts, so it is Theseus's original ship. And the ship in the harbour was made by gradually replacing parts, and replacing a part doesn't make the ship a different ship, so it is also Theseus's original ship. So both ships are his original ship.

Objection: Theseus had only one original ship, so how can both ships be the same as his original ship? The ship in the boatshed and the ship in the harbour are different ships, e.g., we could damage one and the other one wouldn't be damaged. So they can't both be the same as his original ship.

Summary

First, state the question we have discussed: we have been talking about whether something is the same thing once some or all of its parts have been replaced.

Second, summarise what the children have said. The possibilities include:

- It does not matter how many parts are replaced, the ship is still the original ship.
- Even replacing a single part makes the ship a different ship from the original one.
- When all its parts have been replaced, the ship is a different ship from the original one.

Follow up activity

Ask the children to think of more examples of things that have parts that can be replaced, e.g., cars, houses, teddies, clothes, cookers and computers. Ask them to draw one of their examples showing its separate parts, or to write a story about it (e.g., a story about how a car keeps breaking down, and first its wheels are replaced, then its engine, etc). Ask them whether, once all its parts are replaced, it is the same thing.

Alternative version

The enquiry can be done in the same way using toy diggers or cars that come apart into three or four pieces.

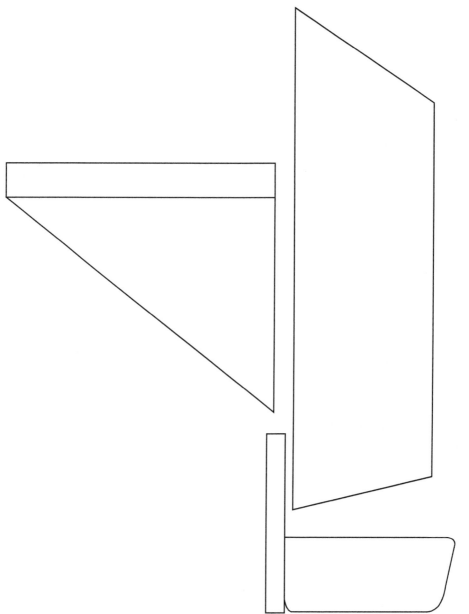

Template for Theseus's ship

Further Reading

Philosophy

Simon Blackburn, *Think! A Compelling Introduction to Philosophy*, Oxford: Oxford University Press, 1999.

> This is a clearly written, fairly advanced introduction, which includes detailed discussion of epistemology, philosophy of mind and ethics, and has a chapter on reasoning.

Thomas Nagel, *What Does it All Mean? A Very Short Introduction to Philosophy*, New York: Oxford University Press, 2004.

> This is a short, engaging read that focuses on philosophical questions and stimulates the reader to think. It is an excellent starting point for learning how to do philosophy.

Nigel Warbuton, *Philosophy: The Basics*, 4th edition, London: Routledge, 2004.

> This is a useful and widely used introduction to the main areas of philosophy, including ethics, political philosophy, epistemology, philosophy of mind and aesthetics.

Philosophy for children

Philip Cam, *Thinking Together: Philosophical Inquiry for the Classroom*, Alexandria, New South Wales: Hale & Iremonger, 1995.

> This book gives some very useful, practical advice about how to run philosophical enquiries.

Robert Fisher, *Teaching Thinking: Philosophical Enquiry in the Classroom*, 2nd edition, London: Continuum, 2003.

> This book discusses the theory, as well as the practice, of philosophy for children.

Thomas Wartenberg, *Big Ideas for Little Kids: Teaching Philosophy through Children's Literature*, Lanham, Maryland: Rowman & Littlefield, 2009.

> Written in a very readable style by a professor of philosophy, this book gives some background to philosophy for children, lots of good general advice and contains eight enquiries using children's books.